George Orwell Studies

Volume One

No. 2

George Orwell Studies

Publishing Office
Abramis Academic
ASK House
Northgate Avenue
Bury St. Edmunds
Suffolk
IP32 6BB
UK

Tel: +44 (0)1284 700321
Fax: +44 (0)1284 717889
Email: info@abramis.co.uk
Web: www.abramis.co.uk

Copyright
All rights reserved. No part of this publication may be reproduced in any material form (including photocopying or storing it in any medium by electronic means, and whether or not transiently or incidentally to some other use of this publication) without the written permission of the copyright owner, except in accordance with the provisions of the Copyright, Designs and Patents Act 1988, or under terms of a licence issued by the Copyright Licensing Agency Ltd, 33-34, Alfred Place, London WC1E 7DP, UK. Applications for the copyright owner's permission to reproduce part of this publication should be addressed to the Publishers.

© 2017 George Orwell Studies & Abramis Academic

ISSN 2399-1267
ISBN 978-1-84549-705-7

George Orwell Studies

Contents

Editorial
Sniffing Out a New Kind of Orwellian Research? – by Richard Lance Keeble — Page 3

Article
It Happened in Burma…Or did it? – by Ron Bateman — Page 7

Papers
The Architecture of Visibility: Blitzed Modernism in Orwell's *Nineteen Eighty-Four* – by Lisa Mullen — Page 13

Beyond the Common Toad: The Animal in Orwell – by Charlie Salter — Page 29

C. L. R. James, George Orwell and 'Literary Trotskyism' – by Christian Høgsbjerg — Page 43

Reviews
Peter Stansky on John Sutherland's *Orwell's Nose: A Pathological Biography*; Luke Seaber on Jürg R. Schwyter's *Dictating to the Mob: The History of the BBC Advisory Committee on Spoken English*; John Newsinger on Jim Smyth's *Cold War Culture: Intellectuals, the Media and the Practice of History*; and Andrew Glazzard on Phyllis Lassner's *Espionage and Exile: Fascism and Anti-Fascism in British Spy Fiction and Film* — Page 61

Editors
John Newsinger — Bath Spa University
Richard Lance Keeble — University of Lincoln

Reviews Editor
Luke Seaber — University College London

Production Editor
Paul Anderson — University of Essex

Editorial Board
Kristin Bluemel — Monmouth University, New Jersey
Tim Crook — Goldsmiths, University of London
Peter Marks — University of Sydney
Marina Remy — Paris Sorbonne
Jean Seaton — University of Westminster
Peter Stansky — Stanford University, US
D. J. Taylor — Author, journalist, biographer of Orwell
Florian Zollmann — Newcastle University

EDITORIAL

Sniffing Out a New Kind of Orwellian Research?

RICHARD LANCE KEEBLE

It has always been striking how, in Orwellian scholarship, the focus has been as much on the man as on his writings. In fact, just months after he died at the tragically early age of 46 in January 1950, a special issue of the Edward Hulton magazine, *World Review*, was devoted to Orwell. Interestingly, the journal mixed both celebration and critique. Orwell's personality as much as his writings clearly fascinated many – and this is reflected in the articles.

Around selections from Orwell's 'Notebooks' (from 18 May 1940 to 28 August 1941), which lie at the core of the journal, are contributions from a glittering array of (all male) journalists and intellectuals: Bertrand Russell, Tom Hopkinson, Aldous Huxley, John Beavan, Herbert Read, Malcolm Muggeridge and Stephen Spender. *World Review* described itself as 'a monthly devoted to literature and the arts and all other aspects of our cultural interests'. It had previously published Orwell's 'Appendix on Newspeak' from his dystopian novel *Nineteen Eighty-Four* (then shortly to be published) though without any background explanation.[1]

Orwell's *Tribune* colleague T. R. Fyvel contributes a 13-page biography. It is split into seven sections: after a brief Introduction, the second section is a moving, personal memoir of his time visiting Orwell in hospital just before he died. He writes (p. 7): 'In this private ward, a square pane of glass is let into the door of each private sickroom, through which patient and caller can see each other. I visited him fairly often during these months, and my first glimpse of him was always through this glass, and always a slight shock, at the sight of his thin, drawn face, looking ominously waxen and still against the white pillow.'

In the final section (pp 18-20), Fyvel returns to personal reminiscences. 'It was probably my second or third encounter with him which remained in my memory. It was at his small mews flat near Baker Street, in London, a rather poverty-stricken affair of one or two rather bare, austere rooms with second-hand furniture. I saw an extremely tall, thin man, looking more than his years, with gentle eyes and deep lines that hinted at suffering on his face.' Following publication of *Animal Farm* in 1945, to 'instantaneous success, especially in America', Orwell, for the first time in his life, became 'comparatively well off'. 'But I found him in character quite unchanged – and physically very tired. … In spite of his many new friendships, he remained a solitary and a lonely man.'

Fyvel later comments (p. 13): 'In personal affairs, Orwell was always extraordinarily reticent, so shy as to be almost secretive. Though he seemed to like to deal in personal asides, e.g."When I was fourteen or fifteen I was an odious little snob", this was always in terms of social classification: the self-revelation is only apparent. In his novels, on the other hand, he himself stands out; for, if he had sharp power of insight, he had much less of invention. From Flory, in his first novel, *Burmese Days*, to Winston Smith in *1984* [as the novel is consistently called throughout the journal, rather than *Nineteen Eighty-Four*], his last, all his heroes are Orwell himself, suitably transmuted.'

John Beavan, who next examines *The Road to Wigan Pier* (pp 48-51), was London editor at the time of the *Manchester Guardian*. Little did he know that he featured on Orwell's infamous 'little list' of crypto-communists handed over to the government's newly formed secret propaganda outfit, the Information Research Department, in 1949. There is an attempt to understand Orwell's complex attitudes to class: 'As a child he was taught that the poor were dirty and immoral and he was denied their society, though they seemed to him to be the most interesting and friendly of people. He never quite got over this.' And Beavan ends: 'Orwell produced at least one book that touched men of his time deeply, and that even his slenderest writings helped many of us to examine our consciences with something of his fierce honesty.'

Poet Stephen Spender, in his short article on *Homage to Catalonia* (pp 51-54), also takes the opportunity to comment on his personality: 'He was perhaps the least Etonian character who has ever come from Eton. He was tall, lean, scraggy man, a Public House character, with a special gleam in his eye, and a home-made way of arguing from simple premises, which could sometimes lead him to radiant common sense, sometimes to crankiness.' On *Homage*, Spender (p. 53) says that it had encouraged him to reflect on the meaning of the phrase 'the living truth'. 'This has all too often in history been exploited in order to trample on human freedoms for the sake of some authoritarian teaching which is supposed to bring happiness in this world or the next. Orwell was extremely sceptical of the claim of any cause to represent "the living truth". But he himself in his own life was an example of "the lived truth", which is perhaps the most valuable truth anyone can offer to humanity.'

The fascination with Orwell the man finds one of its most remarkable expressions in John Sutherland's recently published *Orwell's Nose: A Pathological Biography*, reviewed in this issue of *George Orwell Studies* by Peter Stansky. Sutherland begins by telling us that his interest in Orwell's 'smell narratives' (as he calls them) began a few years ago when he lost his sense of smell. So in a 39-page Preface, Sutherland proceeds to write what could be considered a highly original and witty academic paper exploring the role of smell in Orwell's *oeuvre*. But there is no stopping him. Next (pp 51-250) comes Sutherland's stab at a brief biog of the celebrated writer of *Nineteen Eighty-Four*. Tagged on to the end comes an appendix presenting an imaginary Orwellian 'smoking diary' (which ideally could have been integrated into the Preface) and a close analysis of the 'smell narrative' of the 1935 novel *A Clergyman's Daughter*.

As Professor Stansky points out in his review, Sutherland presents some useful insights. For instance, he points out that his friend, Dennis Collings, who was studying anthropology at Cambridge, told Orwell about Malinowski and being a participant-observer. 'This may well have helped inspire Orwell to go down and out in order to acquire material to write about.'

Moreover, approaching Orwell from quirky, 'oblique, self-indulgent angles' (in Sutherland's own words) can lead to some intriguing new perspectives. On his time serving in Burma with the Imperial Police Service between 1922 and 1927, Sutherland suggests Orwell was essentially an intelligence officer: 'The Burmese police force, like its parent Indian forces, was not primarily an instrument for maintaining law and order but one for gathering intelligence and nipping any possible uprising in the bud. Internal espionage ("IPS is Watching You") was its reason for being'! (pp 104-105). He continues: 'He was not moved around because he gave dissatisfaction but because he was good at his job: a competent spy in policeman's uniform. He was shrewd, fluent in native languages and observant, and could write the kind of clear English that made for a good analytic report' (p. 105).

But the references at the end of the *Nose* indicate only a limited look at the vast literature on Orwell (for instance, Beci Dobbin's essay 'Orwell's squeamishness' in *Orwell Today*, 2012 pp 62-78 would have been a useful resource). And, in the absence of deeply-delving research, Sutherland is left following hunches, raising (often meaningless) questions – and, at worst, spreading scurrilous gossip.

For instance, on page 43 he describes Orwell's second wife, Sonia Brownell, as a 'gratifyingly easy lay' (allegedly Connolly [editor of *Horizon*] would pimp her out to potential backers of his magazine). On page 53, he wonders: 'Did Richard Blair [Orwell's father] console himself with native women in the long years of absence from his family?' He even suggests (p. 55) that Orwell may have witnessed or heard behind closed bedroom doors his father's 'attempts to reclaim "conjugal right", that male right to legally rape an uncooperative spouse'. Of Orwell's friend Brenda Salkeld, he writes (p. 59): '… the surmise is that she never slept with him, despite his urgent requests.' Of Mrs Wilkes, his teacher and tormentor at St Cyprian's prep school, he wonders whether 'she may have been menopausal in Blair's last years at the school' (p. 67). These peculiar sexual preoccupations and speculations continue throughout the text: on page 77, he writes: 'Orwell surely masturbated. Boys' schools, then and now, floated on a sea of frustrated juvenile sperm.' And so on.

The *Nose*, then, is a deliberately provocative, fascinating feast of racy writing and Orwellian musings: a spiffing wheeze celebrating Orwell as the super-sniffer and 'virtuoso of the nostrils'. But does it provide a dangerous precedent for a new kind of Orwellian research in which speculation, rumour, hunches and lurid gossip take precedence over detailed, insightful analysis and investigation?

NOTE

[1] See http://www.orwellsociety.com/world-review-a-magazine-recommended-by-orwell/

ARTICLE

It Happened in Burma...
Or did it?

RON BATEMAN

While Orwell once said that Somerset Maugham was the novelist who had influenced him the most, he wrote very little else about him. Ron Bateman explores this paradox.

In a short autobiographical note to the editors of a publication titled *Twentieth Century Authors* in 1940, George Orwell conceded that William Somerset Maugham was the writer who had influenced him the most, the writer he admired 'with least reserve', citing his ability to tell a good story 'without frills'. Astonishingly, for an author who revelled in the discipline of critically analysing other writers' work, he wrote no essay on Maugham, and in the course of his work generally, he seems to have left Maugham well alone.

Orwell's only known solid reference to Maugham's work in *The Road to Wigan Pier* (1962 [1937]: 120-121) quotes Maugham from his travelogue *On a Chinese Screen* (1922). This is the passage in which Maugham makes the assertion that 'the lower classes smell', leading Orwell to describe how he himself had been *raised to believe* that the lower classes smell, a recollection that commentators regularly mis-read and accused Orwell of harbouring the same belief. Aside from this, one only has to thumb through the index to *The Complete Works* (*CWGO* 20 1998) to confirm that nowhere in the remainder of Orwell's entire *oeuvre* does Maugham merit any real mention of note. Even casual references to Maugham are surprisingly rare for someone whom he so admired and who so clearly influenced his writing style. The earlier Orwell biographers make only two or three references to Maugham at best, while Michael Shelden's *'Authorised' Biography* (1991) doesn't mention him at all.

More recently, Maugham has become a writer of significant interest to scholars reading Orwell, particularly since the appearance of Gordon Bowker's biography *George Orwell* in 2003. Bowker makes no less than sixteen references to Maugham, and even goes so far as to suggest that, in late 1922 or early 1923, Orwell and Maugham were highly likely to have met in Mandalay while the former was at the Imperial Military Police Training School at Fort Dufferin, and while the latter was passing through Burma *en route* to Indo-China (Bowker 2003: 79). The dates are somewhat problematical because Orwell was still very early in his training when Maugham 'passed through', and no evidence has ever been discovered to prove such a suggestion. However, Bowker's style of biography should not be criticised merely for putting forth the likelihood; Bowker is merely stating a hypothesis based on certain probability factors and, in doing so, indirectly invites his readers to put his theory to the test. I, for one, believe that there are clues that the two men did meet in Burma, and may have corresponded or encountered one-another in later life.

Where may such clues that indicate a measure of interaction between the two writers lie? To begin with, Orwell wrote extensively about hop-picking in Kent in both his essay *Hop-Picking* (1931) and in his novel *A Clergyman's Daughter* (1935). This was something Maugham (who spent much of his childhood in Kent) had already previously undertaken in great detail in his most famous novel *Of Human Bondage* (1915). Moving forward, there are elements in the plot of Orwell's *Burmese Days* (1934) that bear a striking resemblance to a short story of Maugham's titled *Force of Circumstance*, first published in *International Magazine* in February 1924. In Maugham's story, set in a remote outpost of the British Empire, the lonely colonial official named Guy succumbs to his unfulfilled sexual instincts and takes on a concubine, the consequences of which, ultimately, ruin his marriage when he returns from leave to settle down in the far-flung province with Doris, his new white European wife.

At the time Maugham was alleged to have met Orwell, the former was already flushed with success and extensively well-travelled and, importantly, he deliberately solicited the life stories of the people he met on his travels. This was the method Maugham always fell back on when attempting to find new ideas for plots and themes in his work. Shortly after returning from Burma, his mind had clearly settled on the custom of concubinage – white men living with native mistresses, as the theme for *Force of Circumstance*. Maugham had discovered that concubinage – a notable exception to the policy of racial separateness before the Great War – was now causing huge problems for the officials administering the British Empire. Previously, so few European women had been prepared to endure the hardships of the East, but now an era of post-war prosperity saw European women regularly going out to live in remote outposts of the British Empire to be with their husbands. How many of these women were profoundly shocked when learning of the existence of their partners' former Asian mistresses and sometimes even children?

How likely is it that a writer who admired Maugham's work such as Orwell would have hit upon the same theme himself? Orwell had finally begun the formal process of writing *Burmese Days* between 1931 and 1933, long after he had discharged himself from imperial service, Even if we accept the claims contained in a recorded interview with Orwell's former colleague George Stuart (Orwell Archive) that the rough draft of *Burmese Days* was written in Burma in 1927, it is still three or four years after *Force of Circumstance* had been published. None of Orwell's former colleagues, or the people who met him in Burma, ever remembered seeing him with a woman. We are told he never went to dances, never liked music and generally stayed in his room and read. Brenda Salkeld, who first met Orwell in Southwold in 1928 and remained a close friend throughout his life, tells us that Orwell never really liked women and once told her that it 'stuck in his throat to have to praise their work' (Coppard and Crick 1984: 68).

In Orwell's defence, the fact that he once conceded to friends that he frequently visited brothels in Rangoon is significant. The likelihood was discussed by Dione Venables recently in *The Complete Poetry*, in which she puts forth the view that 'his enjoyment of their company resounds throughout his verse' (Venables 2015: 20). This calls into question Bernard Crick's earlier dismissal in *George Orwell: A Life* that Orwell's 'claim' is simply a young man 'trying to keep his end up' (Crick 1982 [1980]: 160). Aside from the speculation, the similarities are an interesting case for discussion, simply because in Orwell's first two novels there are specific themes that are present in hugely successful examples of Maugham's earlier work. If it was a case of plot-borrowing, could this instance, followed by the extensive passage on hop-picking in his next novel, have been a source of irritation to Maugham who would have made his feelings known? We know that Orwell valued letters from writers of significance, particularly from the anger he displayed when a letter from H. G. Wells, in response to Orwell's 1941 essay 'Wells, Hitler and the World State' (in which Wells calls Orwell a 'shit') was destroyed. Knowing this, one would have expected any Orwell/Maugham correspondence to have survived unless, of course, he felt either a measure of guilt or that any such correspondence could have damaged him if it fell into the wrong hands.

WAS MAUGHAM'S LARRY DURRELL BASED ON ORWELL?

On Maugham's side, he freely admitted that all of his fictional characters were based on real people he had met, with the exception of Charles Strickland, a character he based on the artist Paul Gauguin whom he researched diligently for his novel *The Moon and Sixpence* (1919). If, indeed, the two men did meet in Burma as

RON BATEMAN

Bowker suggests, it is tempting to assume that the two met again in later life, and that Maugham may have gained something from Orwell to his own benefit. Among Maugham's most successful later works was the novel *The Razor's Edge* (1944) which takes the form of a memoir of an extraordinary individual Maugham met to whom he gave the name Larry Durrell.

The parallels between the actions of Durrell and post-Burma Orwell are striking to say the least. Both men emerged from military service in poor health and somewhat disturbed by the events they had witnessed. Larry's desire to simply 'loaf' thereafter is mirrored in Orwell's reluctance to find a job and just hang around Southwold gathering his thoughts and getting under his parents' feet. One remembers the deeply-scrutinised film of a forlorn-looking figure (believed to be Orwell) ambling down the street in Reydon (near Southwold) on the day the circus came to town.[1]

We know from Orwell that, like Larry Durrell, he was suffering from feelings of guilt, struggling to understand something much deeper within himself – his social conscience. Larry's feelings of guilt are much more poignant as they relate to his friend who had died saving his life during the Great War. He returns from the war a changed man and politely refuses the lucrative offer of a city job guaranteed to endow him with considerable wealth. Thereafter, he sets out upon a path towards finding answers to a multitude of questions, way beyond the understanding of those around him who struggle in their efforts to 'reach' him. Although Orwell did relent temporarily to take on his hated teaching roles, the shared desire deeply embedded within both men was to submerge themselves down into the 'underworld' of the working class, to try to discover something that was up until that point undiscoverable owing to their higher stations in life.

From here onwards the parallels come together almost as one. Just as Orwell went down a coalmine in 1936 to gather material for *The Road to Wigan Pier*, Maugham's character decides to go down a coal mine also in an effort to understand the day-to-day graft of the coal miner (Maugham incidentally arranged to be taken down a coalmine on the outskirts of Paris in 1939 when planning the novel). Larry also strikes up a friendly relationship with a foreigner, just as Orwell does with Boris, while 'down and out' in Paris, and the two of them travel through Germany slumming it and stealing food while trying to get work as farm-labourers. All the while Larry is 'down and out', he still has access to his 'three thousand a year' just as Orwell could get money, a good meal and a comfortable bed whenever he needed it – thanks to the support from his aunt, Nelly Limouzin.

One final interesting parallel is this: before he left Burma, Orwell used to visit regularly the Hpongyi Kyaung (Burmese temple) and converse in very high-flown Burmese with the Hpongyis, or priests – whether for research or spiritual purposes we cannot say. He once commented on his frustration with the Buddhist monks he met there, describing them as all 'too political'. In *The Razor's Edge*, Durrell in the end takes himself off to mystical India where he discovers among the yoga gurus and elder philosophers the kind of spiritual awakening he has always sought.

After *The Razor's Edge* was released in 1944, Maugham conceded that he had had the character of Larry Durrell in mind for around twenty years, which would have been at around the time he allegedly met Orwell. A second trip to India in 1938 re-awakened his interest. Widely regarded as Maugham at his best, *The Razor's Edge* was a huge success, yet critics regarded the 'cardboard character' of Larry Durrell as the book's only flaw, finding him unconvincing, dull, smug and sexless (Hastings 2009: 472). While I would never overplay this parallel, and accept that it could just as easily be explained as mere coincidence, I would suggest that if we are to accept 'likelihoods' in biography – the assertion that a thing 'probably happened' – then it is always worthwhile to go in search of supporting material, particularly if we consider that particular likelihood to be irresistible as, indeed, Bowker does.

One final passage of note in *The Razor's Edge* finds Maugham in a seedy, low-down Paris bar, conversing with Durrell until the early hours; the older, wiser man offering the soul-searching younger man the benefit of his experience and wisdom. The bar is crammed full with the flotsam and jetsam of Paris life – drunks, prostitutes, pimps, failed and wannabe writers and artists, exactly the kind of place Orwell would have frequented when labouring in the Paris restaurants he described in *Down and Out in Paris and London* (1933). The temptation to believe in the possibility of a further meeting is again set before us. Do I truly believe that Durrell was based partly on Orwell? Probably not, but Maugham left few clues as to Durrell's true identity, and there are too many similarities to dismiss it out of hand.

MAUGHAM'S SECRET LIFE

The search for answers would be daunting to say the least, because Maugham as a subject is highly problematical for any biographer. It is known that in his later years, Maugham was fiercely opposed towards any approaches by friends and scholars wishing to write his biography. He requested of his trusted secretary and lover Alan Searle that he should burn every scrap of paper or letters relating to his life so that anyone insistent on betraying his wishes would have very little to go on (Hastings 2009: 513). Aside from this, Maugham lived on into his nineties and so outlived most of his closest acquaintances, meaning that when biographies did appear, there were too few persons left alive to be relied on for first-hand information, particularly about that crucial inter-war period when the 'likely meeting' with Orwell would have taken place.

There is also the question of Maugham's homosexuality at a time when the practice was deemed illegal. More than once, Maugham was warned that he risked being arrested and publicly humiliated, with the result being that he became extremely guarded by nature. Instances of Orwell's perceived homophobia, about which Bowker refers to frequently, are of little significance here, as Orwell had many friends and acquaintances who were homosexual. We can also ascertain from the few biographies that appeared following Maugham's death that, even at a time when he became the most successful writer in the world, he was not popular among critics or contemporaries who denied him the awards and honours he richly deserved. On the occasion of his eightieth birthday, a book of essays on Maugham commissioned by Heinemann was abandoned because the requests were rebuffed by all but two of the twelve authors. Taking all these factors into consideration, we can comfortably assume that evidence of interaction could only realistically arise on Orwell's side as unknown, or unpublished, correspondence of his does occasionally come to light. Orwell did include *The Razor's Edge* on his reading list for 1949, but nothing containing any comment he may have made about it has been uncovered.

Detailed research on Orwell is now well-trodden ground. With every known word that he wrote at our fingertips, we can but sit tight and hope something will turn up that could further illuminate the Orwell/Maugham relationship

NOTE

[1] See Taylor, D. J. (2003) *The Real George Orwell* (extract) *The South Bank Show*. Available online at https://www.youtube.com/watch?v=s3UChbst-j8, accessed on 15 October 2016

REFERENCES

Orwell, G. (1962 [1937]) *The Road to Wigan Pier*, London: Penguin

Bowker, G. (2003) *George Orwell*, London: Little, Brown

Venables, D. (2015) *The Complete Poetry*, London: Finlay Publishers

Coppard, A. and Crick, B. (1984) *Orwell Remembered*, London: Ariel Books/ BBC

Crick, B. (1982 [1980]) *George Orwell: A Life*, London: Penguin

Hastings, S. (2003) *The Secret Lives of Somerset Maugham*, London: John Murray

NOTE ON THE CONTRIBUTOR

Ron Bateman is a founder member of the Orwell Society. He was appointed honourable secretary during the society's formative years before taking on the editorship of the society's *Journal* from 2011 until April 2016. He has since relocated overseas, and now lives in Paciano, Italy.

The Architecture of Visibility:
Blitzed Modernism in Orwell's *Nineteen Eighty-Four*

LISA MULLEN

In constructing his vision of the future in Nineteen Eighty-Four, *Orwell chose not to invent a glassy world of the imagination, but to tether his dystopia to the grimy realities of 1940s London. The novel's concern about the abolition of privacy and autonomy had its roots in contemporary architecture as well as contemporary politics: both the utopian modernist buildings of the 1930s, and the cracked-open buildings that he witnessed during World War Two suggested to him that lives were being exposed to a new kind of unwelcome scrutiny. This paper traces Winston Smith's dissent from the scopic hegemony of Big Brother via his quest for dissident spaces within a city fatally distracted by the totalising discourses of fascism. It situates* Nineteen Eighty-Four *within broader twentieth-century debates about buildings, transparency and autonomy.*

Keywords: *Nineteen Eighty-Four*, architecture, modernism, air raids, glass

When Winston and Julia are arrested by the Thought Police in their secret hideaway above a junk shop, they realise how completely they are entangled in the architecture – both material and conceptual – of totalitarianism. This attic is a space where the lovers have believed themselves invisible; Winston thinks of it as an 'inviolate' world, a relic from the pre-revolutionary era like 'a pocket of the past where extinct animals could walk' (*CWGO* 9: 157). Comforted by its crust of old furniture, he has failed to notice its payload of surveillance technology. At the novel's central moment of crisis, the privacy of this room is torn open, revealing the lovers as sex-criminals, thought-criminals and – most devastatingly – as entirely deluded in their belief that privacy is even possible. They are ordered to stand, shivering and naked, while the Party's iron-shod storm troopers invade the room; commands are barked at them from the telescreen which has lurked all along behind an old engraving; they are utterly exposed. This scene cuts to the heart of the novel's delineation of the intimate incursions that totalitarianism makes into individual lives. The contrast between the cosy hideaway which Winston and Julia had thought they had found, and the revelation that they have, in fact, been clearly seen and minutely scrutinised all along, hammers home the fallacy of freedom within an architecture of visibility without transparency, of brutality and power elaborated into scopic structures unilluminated by hope or truth.

Architecturally, Orwell chose not to model his dystopia on the futuristic glassiness of pre-war imagination, and this paper will examine the context of that aesthetic and ideological decision. It will consider three spatial dynamics within *Nineteen Eighty-Four*: the architecture of oversight; the curdled utopianism of bombastic modernism; and the potential dissidence of undisciplined, street-level wandering through a politically encoded cityscape. By assessing the novel's architectural antecedents in the 1930s, examining its references to the contemporary materiality of blitz-damaged London, and tracing its afterlife in the 1950s Brutalism that emerged from the same post-traumatic impulse, we can begin to situate *Nineteen Eighty-Four* within broader twentieth-century debates about buildings, transparency and autonomy.

THE ARCHITECTURE OF TRAUMA

Orwell's grimy, ragged London provocatively contrasts with the crystalline angularity of both the 'vitra-glass' skyscrapers of Aldous Huxley's *Brave New World* (1932), and the glassily transparent municipality of Yevgeny Zamyatin's *We* (1993 [1924]). The latter novel was recommended by Orwell to his *Tribune* readership as 'more relevant to our own situation' (*CWGO* 18: 14) than Huxley's, and his own novel's debt to this precursor is clear. Like *Nineteen Eighty-Four*, Zamyatin's critique of Soviet socialism was constructed on a nightmare of absolute visibility but, unlike Orwell, he describes a society of glass, premised on ideals of mutual openness and communal scrutiny rather than unreciprocated, top-down surveillance: 'We live in broad daylight inside these walls that seem to have been fashioned out of bright air, always on view,' the narrator of *We* records. 'We have nothing to hide from one another' (Zamyatin 1993 [1924]: 18). In contrast to Zamyatin's glass suburbia, Orwell's gloomy, labyrinthine London is presided over by four vast concrete ziggurats, which form a network of command and control but remain entirely opaque to the population below. Indeed, the aesthetic of futuristic shininess is explicitly rejected in the illicit 'Goldstein book' given to Winston by the Thought Police *agent provocateur* O'Brien. 'The world of today is a bare, hungry, dilapidated place compared with the world that existed before 1914,' Winston reads:

> and still more so if compared with the imaginary future to which the people of that period looked forward. In the early twentieth century, the vision of a future society unbelievably rich, leisured,

orderly and efficient – a glittering antiseptic world of glass and steel and snow-white concrete – was part of the consciousness of nearly every literate person (*CWGO* 9: 196).

Indeed, in 1925 Le Corbusier had outlined a programme for achieving just such a world; his plan for the Marais district of Paris imagined sweeping away the jumble of narrow streets jammed with traffic and infested with people, where 'human life pullulates' and pedestrians are reduced to 'elbowing their way along' (Le Corbusier 1925). Instead of an environment where 'death threatens us at every step', he promises wide, hygienic vistas cleansed of crowds; out of this depopulated expanse, where 'the air is clear and pure' and 'there is hardly any noise', rise 'widely spaced crystal towers which soar higher than any pinnacle on earth'. In these 'translucent prisms' made from 'unbroken expanses of glass', the inhabitants will be unencumbered by pangs of conscience about their privilege, enjoying open-air music recitals and refined conversation high up in rooftop gardens, while 'from far off comes the murmur of the quarters of Paris that remain encrusted in their secular mould'.

In his essay 'Air War and Architecture', written in the aftermath of the 9/11 attack on the World Trade Center in New York, Anthony Vidler points out that Le Corbusier's ideal of visibility was always based on an aerial view, with aeroplanes as the ultimate harbingers of his streamlined and functional aesthetic. 'Le Corbusier even inserts the shadow of the plane on his aerial perspective of [the] towers,' Vidler points out. 'He was obsessed by planes' (Vidler 2010: 34). According to Vidler's analysis, the air raids of World War Two translated such visions of transparent rationality into a more defensive style after 1945. Radical developments in architecture became possible in the wake of war because large areas of land had been cleared and cleansed of history by the bombers. But instead of utopianism, new buildings expressed a submerged fear which persisted throughout the Cold War and beyond – specifically, an abiding fear of annihilation from the air (ibid: 35).

Vidler's essay does not refer to Orwell, but I suggest that these affective structures also emerge in the discursive architecture of *Nineteen Eighty-Four*; its concern with the annihilation of history, and the ruination of personal autonomy and subjecthood which Winston undergoes, not only express Orwell's fears about a totalitarian future, but refer back to his personal experience of aerial bombardment and the erasure it entailed. 'As I write, highly civilised human beings are flying overhead, trying to kill me,' was how he chose to open his passionate call for the onset of British socialism, *The Lion and the Unicorn: Socialism and the English Genius*, in 1941 (*CWGO* 12: 392). The liberty which he urged his readers to demand implied a rejection of the idea that 'civilisation' would be dictated from the top down, in favour of domestic autonomy personalised from the ground up, which he expressed as 'the liberty to have a home of your own, to do what you like in your spare time, to choose your own amusements instead of having them chosen for you *from above*' (ibid: 394, my italics). This observation links the essay to Orwell's pre-war novel *Coming Up For Air* (1939) which is haunted by its narrator's conviction that air war is imminent. George Bowling ends his disappointing search for the idealised England of his childhood when he witnesses the falling of a bomb, which he believes to be the start of a Nazi air raid, although it turns out to be an RAF practice run gone wrong. At the sound of the bomb's whistling descent, Bowling throws himself to the ground 'like a rat when it squeezes under a door': 'BOOM – BRRRRR! A noise like the Day of Judgement, and then a noise like a ton of coal falling onto a sheet of tin' (*CWGO* 7:233). Later, he visits the bomb site and finds a house with 'its wall … ripped off as neatly as if someone had done it with a knife'. The upstairs room is untouched, with all the furniture and other trappings of everyday life exposed; 'It was just like looking into a doll's house,' he observes (ibid: 235). Downstairs, however, a severed leg, 'with the trouser still on it and a black boot' (ibid), is all that remains of one of the house's occupants, while the body of the greengrocer next door leaves no trace behind, 'not even a trouser-button to read the burial service over' (ibid: 236).

Orwell wanted the trauma of the war to bring on a phase of revolution and rebuilding, but one not predicated on the annihilation of individuality and history; similarly, Vidler describes the agenda of successful post-traumatic architecture as being as much about radical memorialisation and the materialisation of resistance as it is about simple reconstruction. It is when post-war buildings promote a rhetoric of forgetting – as everything in Orwell's Oceania does, by force – that they mute the narratives of resistance and become 'the continuation of war by other means' (Vidler 2010: 30). Like the (proposed but never built) memorials to the World Trade Center that Vidler discusses in his essay, Orwell's towering ministries forbid psychological recuperation by employing the language of 'trauma, unmitigated terror, pathological mental states, tormented screams and sexual fears' (ibid: 31). However, in Oceania, where memory and history have been abolished along with the individual consciousnesses which might have retained and replicated them, this expression of terror, literally built into the apparatus of the state, might, in fact, be the last remaining trace capable of evoking resistance – if only it could be read and understood.

THE ARCHITECTURE OF DISTRACTION

In the novel's opening pages, two architectural modes of totalitarian London are immediately juxtaposed. Looking out of the window of his dilapidated flat in Victory Mansions, Winston first contemplates the grimy fabric of the city that Orwell knew in the 1940s – crumbling Victorian slums and 'bombed sites where the plaster dust swirled in the air and the willowherb straggled over the heaps of rubble' (*CWGO* 9: 5). By placing Winston at an upstairs window looking down on the proletarian districts, Orwell reminds us that he, too, is ineluctably implicated in the vertical hierarchies which will ultimately destroy him. Only then does his gaze shift to encompass the totalitarian aesthetic of the towering ministries, fictional structures – though inspired by Senate House in Bloomsbury – which have been superimposed by Orwell on to the wartime city just as the extremist doctrine of Big Brother has been superimposed on to already existing structures of political authority.

As the only tall buildings in the landscape, the ministries stand out starkly from their low-rise, outmoded surroundings; they are 'startlingly different from any other object in sight … soaring up, terrace after terrace three hundred metres into the air' (*CWGO* 9: 5-6). These towers are not a means of claiming access to light and air, as they were in Le Corbusier's vision of Paris but, instead, set up asymmetries of visibility and scrutiny. It is important that these buildings are hypervisible, because, like the ubiquitous posters of Big Brother, they remind the population that they are being watched. At the same time, though, they are opaque: no one knows exactly what goes on behind their blank facades. While the battered streets silently reference the unsanctioned history of a London that has almost, but not quite, been erased, the ministries declare that the Party's programme of obliteration – pursued through a deliberate regime of planned impoverishment and aerial bombardment – must never cease, and must never be completed. The state's carefully calculated architectural rhetoric pits the might and oversight of the Party against the puniness of life lived on the level of granular individuality.

An 'As I Please' column published in *Tribune* on 28 April 1944 sees Orwell pondering the status of the individual and the idea of privacy under totalitarianism. 'The fallacy is to believe that under a dictatorial government you can be free *inside*,' he wrote, going on to scold the complacent for consoling themselves with the idea that *they* would somehow outwit fascist hegemony by retreating into architectural pockets of private liberty. 'Out in the street the loudspeakers bellow, the flags flutter from the rooftops, the police with their tommy-guns prowl to and fro, the face of the Leader, four feet wide, glares from every hoarding,' he mocks; 'but up in the attics the secret enemies of the regime can record their thoughts in perfect freedom' (*CWGO* 16: 172). As Orwell explains, this is an illusion because, under real fascism, not only private space but the very survival of independent thought is impossible: 'The greatest mistake is to imagine that the human being is an autonomous individual. The secret freedom which you can supposedly enjoy under a despotic Government is nonsense, because your thoughts are never entirely your own. ... It is almost impossible to think without talking' (ibid).

By the time he wrote *Nineteen Eighty-Four*, this myth of the isolated dissident had hardened into the hopeless figure of Winston, the lonely 'last man in Europe', who reaches out desperately to a non-existent network of supposedly like-minded rebels, and is destroyed. Winston is blind while the Thought Police see all; as he later learns, they have been monitoring his furtive *thoughtcrime* for seven years. The arrest scene culminates with his belated insight that it is when the structure of totalitarianism becomes fully visible to you that you are doomed; as Winston sees the kindly old junkshop owner Mr. Charrington transformed into a cold-faced Party apparatchik, it occurs to him 'that for the first time in his life he was looking, with knowledge, at a member of the Thought Police' (*CWGO* 9: 234).

Within the tyrannical architecture of visibility, the telescreens retrofitted into the fabric of every building act as a clever distraction. The screen in Winston's flat appears to have been put in the wrong place, offering him a shallow sanctuary in the alcove where he writes his diary, but like all Winston's feeble assertions of autonomy, this turns out to be an illusion: the alcove is another architectural trap, like the room above the junk shop. The real purpose of the screen is to misdirect the gaze of those who are, in fact, under 360-degree surveillance whether they are aware of it or not. In Oceania, looking away from the endless broadcast of disinformation and propaganda is forbidden. While the state oversees the population, the people must reciprocate by submitting their absolute attention to the telescreens, and to the regime of communal affect they enforce, which requires love and hate on demand. Participation is compulsory; distraction is dissidence. The non-transparent glass of the telescreens disciplines domestic space, making it impossible to 'be free inside'. Like the non-glassy, non-utopian towers housing the ministries, this is a perversion of a modernist idea. When Walter Benjamin described modern architecture as the prototype of the revolutionary relationship between people and the culture of the technological age, it was because a building does not absorb the attention of those who experience it, as an auratic artwork might, but is always processed and understood in 'a state of distraction' by the refracted modern subject (Benjamin 2003: 268). In Oceania, both attention and distraction are carefully harnessed and controlled by the totalitarian system: citizens must pay attention to the all-seeing screens with which they cohabit. But they must not think too clearly about the looming structures of the ministries which would dominate their vision and their thoughts, if only they were capable of paying proper attention to them.

THE ARCHITECTURE OF BROKEN GLASS

In the arrest scene, the shattering of Winston's illusion of invisibility coincides with the smashing of a glass paperweight which he has carried with him as a solid symbol of the material and conceptual heterotopia he believes he can access. This solid lump of glass, enclosing a piece of pink coral, captures Winston's attention as soon as he sees it in the junk shop. Gazing into it, he sees 'a tiny world with its atmosphere complete' (*CWGO* 9: 154), a replica in miniature of the secret attic where he thinks he can 'be free inside'. Yet the glass of the paperweight is really a lens – an analogue of the godlike gaze of those who have engineered Winston's fatal flight from conformity. Winston's pocket world is a magnifying glass which offers up its contents for intense scrutiny rather than hiding them from sight, and when it is smashed open the fascinating pink coral turns out to be as tiny and banal as his nascent autonomy: 'How small, thought Winston, how small it always was!' (ibid: 232). The first thing that Mr. Charrington does when he enters the room is to refer to the smashed glass on the floor: 'His eye fell on the fragments of the glass paperweight. "Pick up those pieces," he said sharply' (ibid: 233). This tidiness reveals the ruthless attention to detail of the Party machine: the totemic object of Winston's abortive bid for cognitive emancipation cannot be allowed to persist in time, even in the form of scattered and meaningless shards.

'Neatly swept up piles of glass' (*CWGO* 12: 267) were, for Orwell, a mundane feature of life during the blitz, and the material fragility of glass is emblematic of the impact that air war had on the transparent utopias of the 1920s and 1930s. Both in reality and in Orwell's imagination, London proved starkly vulnerable to the aerial perspective; in the novel, bombs rain down daily on to Airstrip One, just as they had pelted London during the blitz:

> One fell on a crowded film theatre in Stepney, burying several hundred victims among the ruins. … Another bomb fell on a piece of waste ground which was used as a playground and several dozen children were blown to pieces. … Then a rumour flew round that spies were directing the rocket bombs by means of wireless waves, and an old couple who were suspected of being of foreign extraction had their house set on fire and perished of suffocation (*CWGO* 9: 156).

The utopian ideals of modernist transparency and communality have been blitzed into historical oblivion along with the Victorian streets; when the cityscape is smashed open from above, only fear, suspicion and rumour are exposed. Orwell's wartime diaries reveal his growing sense of the erosion of autonomy that creeps into a population under aerial bombardment. Because individuality is abolished by the bomber's omniscient viewpoint, it is easy for people to become an undifferentiated mass of cowering humanity,

LISA MULLEN

herded about by sirens and clipboard-wielding bureaucrats. Driven into communal shelters underground, they find themselves immersed, even imbricated, into the fabric of the city. Orwell visited bomb shelters several times, apparently out of journalistic curiosity, and was struck by how quickly people had assimilated the norms of their new environment. 'The Tube stations don't now stink to any extent,' he noted in his diary for 1 March 1941:

> The people one sees there are reasonably well found as to bedding and seem contented and normal in all ways – but this is what disquiets me. What is one to think of people who go on living this subhuman life night after night for months, including periods of a week or more when no aeroplane has come near London? (*CWGO* 12: 441).

He notes, too, that visitors 'find Londoners very much changed, everyone very hysterical, talking in much louder tones, etc., etc. If this is so it is something that happens gradually and that one does not notice while in the middle of it, as with the growth of a child' (ibid).

This communal collapse of character reflects the literal collapse of the built environment during the months of the blitz, when society's infrastructure burst apart to expose the once-private, and to generalise the once-particular. Another entry from Orwell's diary records 'nondescript people wandering about, having been evacuated from their houses because of delayed-action bombs. Yesterday two girls stopped me in the street, very elegant in appearance except that their faces were filthily dirty. "Please, sir, can you tell us where we are?"' (ibid: 267).

THE ARCHITECTURE OF HYGIENE

It was this general sense of dirt and dislocation that prompted the government to issue a series of propaganda posters, designed by Abram Games, which were intended to re-situate the viewer within the familiar cognitive landscape of progress. Captioned 'Your Country – Fight for it Now!', the posters deliberately echoed pre-war architectural utopianism by reasserting the stark binary of hygienic modernity versus gloom and squalor. In each case, bright, colourful representations of 1930s modernism are shown springing up from the mess and ruin of bombed-out slums, like signposts to a better tomorrow. Nevertheless, these ideal buildings are depicted as scaled-down illustrations pasted on to flat billboards, while the grimy reality they attempt to obscure remains insistently three dimensional in the background (Games 1990: 27).

The choice of buildings carried a message of social justice as well as aesthetic superiority. The most famous of the three posters shows Berthold Lubetkin's Finsbury Health Centre, built in 1936 (Davey

2009). 'Nothing is too good for ordinary people,' declared Lubetkin at the opening, and his building was already well known as a seminal piece of pre-war UK modernism by the time the posters were distributed in 1944. Finsbury pioneered the provision of much-needed free healthcare to an impoverished population; arguably, it was the Finsbury model which was extrapolated into the National Health Service after the war. Like the Games posters, Lubetkin's publicity materials contrasted scenes of antiquated grubbiness with the clean rationality of modern design: 'Large continuous windows give plenty of light,' one caption emphasised, adding somewhat optimistically: 'Glazed tiles, glass facing and windows [are] easily cleaned by means of special cradles' (ibid). This was architecture with both a practical purpose and a political agenda. Its light-filled spaces were designed to induct the slum-dwelling citizens of the local area into a white-tiled future where antisocial impurities had nowhere to hide. An article in *The Lancet* noted approvingly not only the 'wall of glass bricks' at the front of the building but the 'disinfecting station and cleansing station' with its 'high-pressure steam apparatus' (*Lancet* 1938). At the opening, 'visitors expressed horror at the thought of children actually having scabies or harbouring nits, but could not help admiring the arrangements by which a child and its clothes were cleaned and returned to sender within an hour'.

For Orwell, though, the Finsbury centre's regime implied an intolerable constriction of individual autonomy; in *The Road to Wigan Pier*, published a year after the opening of Finsbury, he wrote about such sterilisation procedures as 'the kind of thing that makes you wish the word "hygiene" could be dropped out of the dictionary. Bugs are bad, but a state of affairs in which men will allow themselves to be dipped like sheep is worse' (*CWGO* 5: 67). In *Nineteen Eighty-Four*, Finsbury's cleansing stations and ultraviolet sunlamps are transformed into the Ministry of Love's windowless hell, where unrelenting electric light becomes an ideological disinfectant. O'Brien has promised Winston that they will meet in 'the place where there is no darkness' (*CWGO* 9: 185), but the Ministry of Love is no glass-bricked temple to health and sunshine, but a high-tech dungeon that uses light as torture.

The modernist rhetoric of progressive sunshine was similarly evoked in Games's second poster, which showed Impington Village College in Cambridgeshire, built in 1939 and designed by Maxwell Fry and his mentor Walter Gropius (Games 1990: 27). In this vision of a future worth fighting for, neat, attentive children can be seen through floor-to-ceiling plate-glass windows, while in the shabby 'real' world a gloomy and derelict school room is populated only by a broken desk and a tattered poster of the beleaguered British Isles. When the school opened in 1939, *The Times* published a report which praised its 'walls which are virtually windows' (*Times*

1939) but, nevertheless, struck a distinctly reactionary note by emphasising the firmly-circumscribed ambitions of its implied community of users. The school's 'less academic curriculum' was congratulated for emphasising 'the skills which make for a happy and healthy family life' and for teaching only 'the scientific knowledge and practice essential to the young countryman'. The opening ceremony, meanwhile, had an almost fascistic air: '… boys stripped to the waist gave an exhibition of agility exercises which the Nazis would call *Wehrsport*; girls performed rhythmic exercises to music.' 'The library is being used with enthusiasm,' it was noted, 'and there was a long list of applications for *Mein Kampf*.' In all, the unnamed correspondent concluded, the college offered both the 'normal unacademic boy and girl' and the 'ordinary man and woman' a limited chance to experience 'what life can be like in a building and society dedicated to the culture of body and mind', but there is little enthusiasm for the idea of individual aspiration, let alone social equality with the middle-class readers of *The Times*.

To many, Orwell included, modernism in architecture seemed nothing more than a series of empty gestures towards an uncomfortable and undesirable future. In *Coming Up for Air* (1939), George Bowling is disgusted by the ultramodern, contentless aesthetic of a milk bar which seems to him to embody the idea 'that food doesn't matter, comfort doesn't matter, nothing matters except slickness and shininess and streamlining' (*CWGO* 7: 22). In this, he echoes Wyndham Lewis's disdain for the oxymoron of 'ultra-puritan' luxury, consisting of 'uncompromisingly severe bookcases, rugs, steel chairs and aluminium beds, angular armchairs and so forth' (Lewis 1989: 246-247) which encouraged 'robotic tastes, with an itch for the rigours of the anchorite, and a sentimental passion for metal as opposed to wood, and a super-Victorian conviction that cleanliness is next to godliness' (ibid: 254-255). Clearly, the ambition of Gropius, Fry and Lubetkin to devise an architecture that could resist, or dismantle, class structures did not always yield ideal results.

THE ARCHITECTURE OF RESISTANCE
The residential building which featured on Abram Games's third propaganda poster attempted to answer this charge of modernism as the masochistic affectation of a wealthy elite (Games 1990: 27). Kensal House flats in Ladbroke Grove, designed by Maxwell Fry and built in 1938, was described as 'a community in action', and the building promoted a bracing agenda of communal improvement alongside a predictable commitment to glass bricks. It was built in a curved fishbowl style to enhance the panoptical sense of mutual purpose, and incorporated a community centre, a crèche, a communal laundry and canteen facilities. Residents could attend metalwork and woodwork classes, or join the gardening club, while a specially-built kindergarten allowed children to play in a safe, clean environment, watched by their parents.

In *Nineteen Eighty-Four*, the community ideals of Kensal House have curdled into compulsory *goodthink* and the smell of boiled cabbage. Winston's dissent from the skewering gaze of Big Brother is first expressed by a physical retreat from such enforced communality:

> A Party member had no spare time, and was never alone except in bed. It was assumed that when he was not working, eating, or sleeping he would be taking part in some kind of communal recreation: to do anything that suggested a taste for solitude, even to go for a walk by yourself, was always slightly dangerous. There was word for it in Newspeak: *ownlife*, it was called, meaning individualism and eccentricity (*CWGO* 9: 85).

Winston takes the risky decision to miss an evening at a Party-run community centre which is curiously reminiscent of the one at Kensal House:

> Suddenly the long, noisy evening at the Centre, the boring, exhausting games, the lectures, the creaking camaraderie oiled by gin, had seemed intolerable. On impulse he had turned away from the bus-stop and wandered off into the labyrinth of London, first south, then east, then north again, losing himself among unknown streets and hardly bothering in which direction he was going (ibid: 69).

In his quest for the unlit, dissident spaces of the city, he wanders into the jumbled chaos of the proletarian back streets. During the blitz, Orwell described how unexploded bombs and closed roads made walking home 'like trying to find your way to the heart of a maze' (*CWGO* 12: 263). But here, Winston's wandering has a purposeful purposelessness, like a Situationist act of psychogeographical critique. To wander physically away from the sanctioned spaces of the city is another form of disobedient distraction, like refusing to pay attention to the telescreen. Winston's dérive is not so much 'the path of least resistance' that Guy Debord would describe a few years later (Debord 1955), as the path of *most* resistance: Winston wants to access a new relationship with the tangible fabric of the city, because he hopes he will be able to read there an alternative cultural history of humanity, written in obsolete spaces and objects. Michel de Certeau's post-Foucauldian analysis of urban experience describes a dichotomy between the godlike oversight of the towerblock and the secret inscriptions of street-level reality. He describes the dweller in the skyscraper, like the ever-watchful Big Brother, as 'an Icarus', a 'voyeur' whose elevation 'transforms the bewitching world ... into a text that lies before one's eyes. It allows one to read it, to be a solar Eye, looking down like a god. The exaltation of a scopic and gnostic drive: the fiction of knowledge is related to this lust to be a viewpoint and nothing more' (de Certeau 1984: 92).

LISA MULLEN

This Icarian view is the kind of epistephilic, technologically enhanced knowledge that the Party system wants to promulgate in *Nineteen Eighty-Four*, while Winston wants to be the Daedalus who will find his way through the labyrinth below. But in Orwell's novel, the 'fiction' of total knowledge has become nightmarishly real. For de Certeau, the practice of walking at street level creates narratives and discourses which evade the panoptic gaze, etching personal memories and histories on to the fabric of the city. At first, it seems that this is what Winston is achieving on his forays into the streets, which lead him to the apparent sanctuary of the junk shop. He is in search of his own history and the history of London, both bound together in fragments of memory and architecture, just as stories and places are joined together in the rhyme 'Oranges and Lemons', which he recites with Mr. Charrington and which becomes a kind of shibboleth of his *ownlife* rebellion. However, this rhyme, which memorialises London's churches and turns the pealing of their bells into a song, also tells a dark story about light, and punishment that descends from above without warning: 'Here comes the candle to light you to bed, here comes the chopper to chop off your head' (*CWGO* 9: 102).

During the process of entrapment that guides Winston to his doom, O'Brien suggests that physical integrity may need to be sacrificed by those joining the dissident Brotherhood: 'Our surgeons can alter people beyond recognition,' he says. 'Sometimes it is necessary. Sometimes we even amputate a limb' (ibid: 180-81). O'Brien is offering Winston a fantasy of invisibility based on dismemberment, and his words contain a warning about the true nature of the Brotherhood – a warning that Winston cannot yet hear. A truly socialist collective, like the one Orwell described in *The Lion and the Unicorn* (1941), would prioritise and preserve the identity of the individual, instead of surgically excising it. A dismembered subject can be made to disappear by the ever-watchful Thought Police, just as the 'nondescript' non-persons of the blitzed streets in Orwell's diary were rendered paradoxically invisible by the all-seeing eye of the bomber pilot.

THE ARCHITECTURE OF APOCALYPSE

The end of World War Two seemed to promise the reinstatement of the pre-war privacies which had been suspended while the civilian population was mobilised and militarised. Yet the incursions into private spaces did not abate, but rather shifted in emphasis. In 1946, an exhibition of domestic design at the V & A, *Britain Can Make It*, sought to reframe the idea of blitz communality as a model for techno-futurist consumerism (*Britain Can Make It* 1946). This was really an exercise in counterfactual utopianism, since it showcased new British designs in domestic and industrial goods which existed only in prototype and could not yet be bought. Consciously or otherwise, the exhibition invoked memories of the blitz beyond its punning title, which referenced Humphrey Jennings's blitz-survival propaganda film *Britain Can Take It!* (1940). In wartime, bombs had sliced homes open to reveal private spaces filled with the bric-à-brac of ordinary life; in the exhibition, idealised room-sets presented as-yet-unattainable modern domestic commodities behind a theatrical fourth wall, allowing visitors to spy into the perfectly appointed lives on which they were encouraged to base their new consumer aspirations (Hornsey 2008: 108).

Like Orwell, some post-war architects rejected this capitalist assault on idiosyncrasy and autonomy. 'Can the individual add "identity" to the house, or is the architecture packaging him?' asked Alison and Peter Smithson in their 1957 manifesto *Criteria for Mass Housing* (Smithson, A. and P. 1967: 393). The fortress-like aesthetic of New Brutalism co-opted the concrete of Orwell's overbearing towers, but reimagined it as a protective skin for a resurgent collective, which also memorialised the defensive structures – the pill boxes and gun emplacements – of the recent fight against fascism. The Smithsons' architectural installation *Patio and Pavilion*, which formed part of 1956's *This is Tomorrow* exhibition at the Whitechapel Gallery, distilled this need for an architectural cathexis of trauma. In collaboration with the artists Nigel Henderson and Eduardo Paolozzi, they created a vision of a violated domesticity which echoed Orwell's critique of visibility. It is described by Vidler in his essay as a shack 'surrounded by the detritus of civilisation, the shards of a post-apocalyptic world' (Vidler 2010: 37), but his description tends to overlook the installation's provocative playfulness. It consisted of a porous dwelling, an open-sided shed-like structure with a translucent roof, which was presided over by a giant, watchful face (Walsh 2001: 115). Like Orwell's novel, it represented a riposte to old-style utopianism, and for this reason it was starkly at odds with the architectural optimism of the rest of the exhibition. But *Patio and Pavilion* insists that the city's abandoned and derelict spaces be not only remembered but reinhabited, and their personal stories told.

Indeed, their pavilion was filled by Henderson and Paolozzi with blitz debris picked up from the still-extant wastelands of London, carefully arranged, not as exhibits from a lost civilisation as Vidler would have it, but as if salvaged for reuse. On the wall of the shack, the outsize face that dominates the pavilion recalls the posters of Big Brother, but its lopsided gaze projects benign thoughtfulness rather than oppressive surveillance. Usually assumed to be a self-portrait, this collaged head was created by bomber-pilot-turned photographer Nigel Henderson and is made up, on closer inspection, of fractured scraps and found images which play with the viewer's sense of scale and orientation. Describing a similar work he made in the wake of the war, *Collage 1949*, Henderson wrote: 'It's all, for me, very like the flying experience – the experience of scale – wherein at say 15,000 ft. the terrain takes on an overall unity, identity, that you can selectively break down by diving – by gliding down. This is the action of the microscope and of the enlarger which has such interest for me' (Henderson 1978). Seen as a response to *Nineteen Eighty-Four*, *Patio and Pavilion* expresses the political optimism both of pop art and of New Brutalism: here, the Icarian eye celebrates particularity instead of obliterating it: the installation marries porosity and privacy together, and insists on individual memory as the key to collective redemption.

CONCLUSION

In 'Why I Write' (1946), Orwell defined the proper aspiration of literature as a quest for visibility: 'Good prose,' he wrote, 'is like a windowpane' (*CWGO* 18: 320). Yet, as we have seen, he was troubled by the implications of transparency as it related to the material apparatus of state surveillance. This paper has sought to clarify the ways in which Orwell saw connections between a modernist ideal of mutual transparency and the asymmetric visibility represented by the non-transparent glass telescreens of *Nineteen Eighty-Four*. Whereas Yevgeny Zamyatin had posited a world of crystal clarity in which secrets shrivelled under the multi-directional glare of the community at large, Orwell saw in the glitter of modernist glass – and even in the more modest utopianism typified by the buildings pictured on Abram Games's propaganda posters – a place where the secret impulses of a new kind of totalitarianism might be incubated.

When the air raids of the blitz arrived in a hail of smashed glass, this tension between transparency and visibility would inform the oppressive architectural aesthetic of *Nineteen Eighty-Four*. The lens-like magnification achieved by Winston's junk-shop paperweight could be scaled up into the overbearing oversight achieved by state surveillance operated from soaring concrete ministries, capable of breaking open the illusory privacies of the population below. For Orwell, any lofty perspective which claimed to encompass experience in a single glance was automatically suspect. Winston Smith performs his dissent at street level, making his way out of the disciplined spaces of Party membership in order to lose himself – so he hopes – in the mazelike proletarian districts which he believes have escaped the glassy interventions of modernity. The fact that this escape into the fabric of the old city turns out to be illusory shows that Orwell realised – as Winston did not – that the new scopic technologies were breaking through the material and conceptual defences of the private citizen and demanding submission to transparency by force. In the decade that followed his death, however, a similar disquiet about such overarching scopic hegemony opened up a conceptual space where the New Brutalists could begin to acknowledge and articulate wartime trauma in what might be termed an experiment in post-utopian architecture.

In her magisterial account of the uses of glass in the nineteenth century, Isobel Armstrong pinpoints the way in which its physical materiality complicates the concept of transparency, and distinguishes it from pure and absolute transitivity. Glass offers, according to Armstrong, a 'moment of difficulty', a 'resistant obstruction that requires recognition before the work of rethinking can occur' (Armstrong 2008: 12). Like all materials, glass bears the traces of its manufacture, its historicity, and its potential futures:

> The workman's breath, the grit of sand, the 'double lustre' of glass, its secondary world of reflection, the boundarylessness of glass structures, the ideality of the image, the democratic pleasure principle, and glass's invitation to violence, all call paradoxes and contradictions into play that have to be worked through (ibid).

Orwell's window-pane prose, then, may be just this kind of glass; a site of mediation and resistance, rather than a frictionless conduit for uninflected objectivity. Such a reading helps to resolve the apparent contradiction between the declared intentions of 'How I Write' and the habitual practice of Orwell the observer, the interpreter, and the stylist, who placed himself deliberately and sometimes obtrusively between his raw material and his readership, especially in his journalism and documentary writing.

Discursive transparency was Orwell's essential bulwark against propaganda, obfuscation and the abolition of independent thought; what was at stake was not merely good style, but intellectual survival. Yet he balanced this 'essentially public, non-individual' motivation for writing against a more personal preference for the distractions of 'solid objects and scraps of useless information', declaring that 'it is no use trying to suppress that side of myself' (*CWGO* 18: 320). Transparency should not be the enemy of individuality: for Orwell, the best defence of freedom stems from clear-sighted attentiveness to the grit and the flaws of a palpable, and sometimes grubby, reality. To resist the devastating lens of state oversight, the individual must be tirelessly watchful in turn, alert to collective counter-narratives of decency and common sense that emerge like hidden pathways of resistance through the architecture of totalitarianism.

REFERENCES

Armstrong, Isobel (2008) *Victorian Glassworlds: Glass Culture and the Imagination 1830-1880*, Oxford: Oxford University Press

Benjamin, Walter (2003) The work of art in the age of its technological reproducability (third version), Eiland, Howard and Jennings, Michael W. (eds) *Selected Writings Vol 4. 1938-1940* (trans. Jephcott, Edmund et al.), Cambridge, MA: Belknap Harvard pp 251-270

Complete Works of George Orwell (*CWGO*) (1998) Edited by Davison, Peter, 20 Vols, London: Secker and Warburg

LISA MULLEN

Britain Can Make It Exhibition Guide (1946), London: HMSO

Davey, Peter (2009), Lubetkin's Finsbury Heath Centre – The Ideal that Time Forgot, *BD Online*, March. Available online at http://www.bdonline.co.uk/lubetkin%E2%80%99s-finsbury-health-centre-%E2%80%94-the-ideal-that-time-forgot/3135725.article, accessed on 16 February 2017

Debord, Guy (1955) Introduction to a critique of urban geography, *Les Lèvres Nues* No. 6 (trans. by Knabb, Ken). Available online at http://www.cddc.vt.edu/sionline/presitu/geography.html, accessed on 16 February 2017

de Certeau, Michel (1984) *The Practice of Everyday Life* (trans. by Rendall, Steven), Berkeley: California

Games, Abram (1990) *60 Years of Design*, South Glamorgan: Institute of Higher Education

Henderson, Nigel (1978) Letter quoted in *The Tate Gallery 1974-6: Illustrated Catalogue of Acquisitions*, London: Tate. Available online at http://www.tate.org.uk/art/artworks/henderson-collage-t01915/text-catalogue-entry, accessed on 16 February 2017

Hornsey, Richard (2008) Everything Is Made of Atoms, *Journal of Historical Geography*, Vol. 34 pp 94-117

Le Corbusier (1925) *Plan Voisin, Paris, France*. Available online at http://www.fondationlecorbusier.fr/corbuweb/morpheus.aspx?sysId=13&IrisObjectId=6159&sysLanguage=en-en&itemPos=2&itemCount=2&sysParentName=Home&sysParentId=65, accessed on 16 February 2016

Lewis, Wyndham (1989) Home-builder: Where is your Vorticist?, *Wyndham Lewis: Creatures of Habit and Creatures of Change: Essays on Art, Literature and Society 1914-1956*, Santa Rosa, CA: Black Sparrow Press pp 246-256

Smithson, Alison and Smithson, Peter (1967) Criteria for mass housing, *Architectural Design*, September pp 393-394

Lancet (1938) Something new in Finsbury, 29 October pp 1027-1028

Times (1939) A new village college, 21 December p. 11

Vidler, Anthony (2010) Air war and architecture, Hell, Julia and Schönle, Andreas (eds) *Ruins of Modernity*, Durham and London: Duke University Press pp 29-40

Walsh, Victoria (2001) *Nigel Henderson: Parallel of Life and Art*, London: Thames and Hudson

Zamyatin, Yevgeny (1993 [1924]) *We* (trans. Brown, Clarence), New York and London: Penguin

NOTE ON THE CONTRIBUTOR

Dr Lisa Mullen is the Steven Isenberg Junior Research Fellow at Worcester College, Oxford University, where she is working on a book titled *Orwell Unwell: Pathology and the Medical Imaginary in the Fiction and Journalism of George Orwell*.

PAPER

Beyond the Common Toad:
The Animal in Orwell

CHARLIE SALTER

While we typically associate the term 'Orwellian' with the dystopian nightmare world of Nineteen Eighty-Four, *there is a common thread which plays a more significant role in defining the author's voice: animals and the natural world. When one thinks of George Orwell and animals, his novel* Animal Farm *inevitably comes to mind. However, animals did not just play a part in his famous barnyard fable. Nature is a recurrent theme throughout many of Orwell's works, and populates the pages of both his fiction and journalism. While many other formative factors must be taken into account when trying to interpret the writing and views of this prolific writer, this paper will argue that understanding the significance of this persistent theme is integral in gaining a full understanding of Orwell's works. The paper will draw on contextual analysis of where Orwell's work sits in relation to his literary influences, his personal passion for the natural world, and it will explore how this motif connects his works in surprising ways. The paper concludes that Orwell's tendency to return to nature is a foundational element of his literary voice. This bucolic passion is at the core of many of his works.*

Keywords: Orwell, animals, nature, modernity, fable

ORWELL, ANIMAL ALLEGORY AND *AESOP'S FABLES*

As a metaphorical and allegorical device, animals have played an integral role in writing since the birth of literature. The use of anthropomorphism in literature – that is, ascribing human characteristics and motivations to animals – can be traced back to our early perceptions of animal behaviour. Before the philosopher René Descartes (1596-1650) proposed the now-defunct notion that all non-human animals are machines, lacking a mind or consciousness and hence not sentient beings (Boakes 1984: 85-86), anthropomorphism was often applied when attempting to understand animal behaviour. While it is now viewed as an obsolete approach scientifically, anthropomorphism, as Kennedy argues, can be seen as an inexorable quality of the human condition, both culturally and biologically:

CHARLIE SALTER

...anthropomorphic thinking about animal behaviour is built into us. We could not abandon it even if we wished to. It is dinned into us culturally from earliest childhood. It has presumably also been 'pre-programmed' into our hereditary make-up by natural selection, perhaps because it proved to be useful for predicting and controlling the behaviour of animals (Kennedy 1992: 5).

Given the ingrained nature of anthropomorphism within human history, it is perhaps unsurprising that Orwell, and countless writers before and after him, imparted human characteristics on to animals and used them as an allegorical device. Anthropomorphism is explicitly used in one of Orwell's most well-known works, *Animal Farm* (2003 [1945]).

When exploring the early roots of animals as an allegorical device in literature, it unavoidably leads us back to ancient fables. Perhaps the most defining example of animal allegory is *Aesop's Fables* (1997 [620-564 BCE]). The fables, attributed to a slave who lived in ancient Greece circa 620-564 BCE, have left a firm imprint on modern literature and how writers articulate morality. Most of *Aesop's Fables* employ anthropomorphism in the form of animals (and occasionally gods) with human traits, personality and speech, seeking to expound upon humanity's vices. All of *Aesop's Fables* conclude with a moral lesson, or 'moralitas', and in this sense the allegorical meaning is clearly understood. As Fletcher explains: '…in *Aesop's Fables*, the moral appears to be a clear and unequivocal statement of the allegorical sense, and we come to expect such aids toward clear interpretation' (Fletcher 2012: 310). However, Orwell's use of 'Aesopian' devices differs from its source, abandoning plainly spelling out his allegorical intentions. While to many readers, some of Orwell's allusions are clear, his writing diverges from the established 'nominally unequivocal' (ibid) form of the fable to a morality tale more open to reader interpretation, and more specific to its historical context.

Some characteristics of Aesopian writing are still evident in *Animal Farm*. While more politically specific, the writing style retains the laconic tone of a fable – the novel was, after all, subtitled '*A Fairy Story*'. However, it is said that Orwell selected this subtitle as an ironic joke, implying that the fable was no mere 'fairy story', but that what it describes was really happening in Stalin's Russia, and the book could act as a cautionary tale, suggesting that it could happen anywhere (Rodden 2003: 72). Works of political allegory seem to be linked to the thematic function of 'Aesop language' (Fletcher 2012: 326), and Orwell's writing is clearly no exception to this.

While ancient writings such as *Aesop's Fables* may well have had an impact on Orwell's barnyard tale, his anthropomorphic influences are not limited to literature. As Dickstein says:

Orwell's inspiration came as much from the vogue of animated cartoons in the previous decade, featuring Mickey Mouse, Porky Pig and Donald Duck, as from any literary source (Dickstein 2007: 134-135).

In his biography of Orwell, Bowker claims that J. R. R. Tolkien (whose famous 1937 fairy tale *The Hobbit* is itself a political allegory) would have classed *Animal Farm* as a 'beast fable'. Bowker points out that Tolkien defined the 'beast fable' as one 'in which the animals are the heroes and heroines, and men and women, if they appear, are mere adjuncts' (Bowker 2003: 308). When viewed in the context of classical fables, Orwell's *Animal Farm* is a work which, although sharing their simplistic tone and symbolic narrative, is far more explicit and satirical than its folklore predecessors.

As Aguirre reasons, Orwell's novel is a much more developed iteration of the 'beast fable'. *Animal Farm*, in contrast to *Aesop's Fables*, places the moral emphasis on its plot. However, similarities to more traditional fables can be seen, for instance, in Orwell's fast-paced, straightforward writing style (Aguirre 2016). *Animal Farm* can be seen as distinct from traditional fables in its specific subject matter (an obvious allegory for the history of Soviet communism), as opposed to the general meditations on morality offered by the fables from which it draws its outer aesthetic. Yet, on one level the book can be read as a traditional form of allegory, in which Orwell employs the use of established animal archetypes to tell his story, as Rodden explains:

> *Animal Farm* is an allegory written in the form of a beast fable, in which the misadventures of animals expose human follies. Orwell draws on our cultural stereotypes of animals. Pigs have a bad name for selfishness and gluttony. Horses are slow-witted, strong, gentle and loyal. Sheep are brainless and behave as a flock without individual initiative (Rodden 2003: 72).

The moral lessons from *Aesop's Fables* have had a significant impact on our culture, and have forged many animal archetypes in the lexicon of anthropomorphic animals that would follow. The notion of animals possessing particular traits and characteristics linked to their species is a concept that was drawn upon in many early fables:

> ...the fable tradition frequently expresses the view that everyone – human and animal – has an essential, unchangeable nature, and that it is dangerous to attempt to transcend the limitations of one's character or to try to improve one's natural circumstances (Lefkowitz 2014: 14).

However, while Orwell uses these stereotypes, the symbolism in *Animal Farm* works in a more complex way. Rodden suggests

CHARLIE SALTER

that adhering to the composition of most allegories, *Animal Farm* operates on two contrasting levels, the literal and the symbolic (Rodden 2003: 72). Orwell acknowledges these two elements in his essay 'Why I Write' (2004 [1946]), where he says: '*Animal Farm* was the first book in which I tried, with full consciousness of what I was doing, to fuse political purpose and artistic purpose into one whole' (ibid: 9).

The classical, Aesopian approach to allegory did not just impact on Orwell in terms of the marked anthropomorphism in *Animal Farm*. As Fletcher points out, in *Nineteen Eighty-Four*, the protagonist, Winston Smith, is symbolically reduced to the status of vermin. In likening a human character to vermin, Orwell's famous dystopian novel follows on from the allegorical conventions laid out by its Aesopian and medieval predecessors, who would frequently show man as a species of animal (Fletcher 2012: 142). In *Nineteen Eighty-Four*, Orwell not only compares Winston to vermin, but uses this subject to explore the very nature of depravity. Rats are a recurrent theme in the novel.

DRAWING INSPIRATION FROM *GULLIVER'S TRAVELS* AND *THE WIND IN THE WILLOWS*

Two classic works of literature, Jonathan Swift's *Gulliver's Travels* (1726) and Kenneth Grahame's *The Wind in the Willows* (1908) are essential to consider when understanding Orwell's literary voice. Here I will explore the part they played in inspiring Orwell to develop his distinctive variety of allegory.

Orwell idolised Swift's *Gulliver's Travels*, and once remarked that it was hugely important to him:

> I believe *Gulliver's Travels* has meant more to me than any other book ever written. I can't remember when I first read it, I must have been eight years old at the most, and it's lived with me ever since so that I suppose a year has never passed without my re-reading at least part of it (Orwell 2001 [1998]: 157).

In 1946, Orwell reviewed the book in a critical essay 'Politics vs. Literature: An Examination of *Gulliver's Travels*', in which he argued that it is one of the books that should be preserved above all others (Orwell 1970a [1946]). Orwell was influenced by the third and fourth parts of Jonathan Swift's *Gulliver's Travels* in particular, which were special favourites of his. They provided him with inspiration for writing *Animal Farm* – a fairy tale which attempts to answer the larger questions of human society (Dickstein 2007: 135).

The most immediate connection Swift's tales have to Orwell's works is their use of the animal fable as a method of delivering political satire. While Orwell's politics were at odds with Swift's views, which

Orwell unfavourably described as 'perverse Toryism' (Orwell 1970 [1946]), both used similar methods to articulate their perspectives. Much like *Animal Farm*, *Gulliver's Travels* used anthropomorphism to underline class difference. In *Animal Farm*, much like Swift did before him, Orwell used the animal fable to simplify and universalise his viewpoints. However, Orwell's novel makes it more immediately apparent what his allegory represents. Both Swift and Orwell depict representations of utopia and dystopia, a theme which links many of Orwell's works. While Orwell's *Animal Farm* and *Nineteen Eighty-Four* are more overt vehicles for specific political caveats, they share a narrative similarity:

> *Animal Farm* is a warning, if you like, just as *Nineteen Eighty-Four* is, as well as a fictionalized account of actual happenings, but it also, like *Gulliver's Travels*, a description in narrative form of natural and social forces perennially interacting in an imperfect human world, its central concern being not only with Party but with the old civic morality and its expression in government (Baker-Smith 1987: 93).

Grahame's influential children's novel *The Wind in the Willows* (1908) also matches this duality of fairy tale and moral teaching. In *The Wind in the Willows*, we are presented with a cast of anthropomorphic animals, such as Mole, Rat, Mr. Toad and Mr. Badger, who all live on a picturesque riverbank. *The Wind in the Willows* can be seen as a development of the allegorical foundations laid out by *Aesop's Fables*: 'The animals [in *The Wind in the Willows*] are vehicles for conservative philosophy, just as, in *Aesop's Fables*, they were vehicles for moral teaching' (Fudge 2002: 72). A comparison can, of course, be made to the anthropomorphised characters in *Animal Farm*. Grahame's book was a children's book, and while Orwell's beast fable is intended for an adult audience, both texts are matched by their merging of narrative simplicity and a deeper political meaning (Meyers 2010: 106-107).

Both authors created a hierarchy between the animals, and while *Animal Farm*'s slogan 'ALL ANIMALS ARE EQUAL BUT SOME ANIMALS ARE MORE EQUAL THAN OTHERS' patently underlines this power structure, a similar, yet unspoken, rule applies in *The Wind in the Willows*, in which the stoats become a lower class than the weasels (ibid: 112). While Grahame had an influence on Orwell, it should also be noted that there were other inspirations behind this phrase. The slogan combines Thomas Jefferson's concept in the Declaration of American Independence (of 1776), 'all men are created equal', and Eve's self-destructive command to the Serpent in Milton's *Paradise Lost* (1667), 'render me more equal, and perhaps, / A thing not undesirable, sometime / Superior' (Meyers 2000: 248).

Orwell and Grahame use these techniques to deliver distinctly different viewpoints, and though both fables are counter-revolutionary, Grahame expresses a conservative message, endorsing the class system he depicts, while Orwell expresses his opinion from the standpoint of a critical socialist (ibid: 113). Aside from the fable aesthetic, another concept links Grahame and Orwell's works. In *Animal Farm*, Orwell uses the abortive electric windmill the animals build as an allegory for the negative effects of industrialism. In *The Wind in the Willows*, Grahame communicates a similar sentiment, in the form of Toad's obsession with automobiles.

The theme of a modernity as a menace to rural life, which *The Wind in the Willows* inspired, can also be found in another of Orwell's novels. Just as Orwell used nature and the rural landscape as a device to protest against the threat of modernity in *Coming Up For Air* (2001 [1939]), so too does Grahame in his novel. The riverbank where the animals live on in *The Wind in the Willows* represents an idealised picture of human society, with Mr. Toad abandoning this way of life, tempted by a motorcar. The motorcar itself is an allegory for the disintegration of the rural lifestyle, and the threatening arrival of modernity (Fudge 2002: 71). In his novel *Coming Up For Air*, Orwell uses the modernisation of the protagonist's rural home town to a similar end. As Meyers observes, while Orwell and Grahame had differing political views, *Coming Up For Air* and *The Wind in the Willows* are linked by a prevailing nostalgia for the days of old:

> The hero of his novel *Coming Up For Air* (1939), like Grahame's characters, longs to escape from the harsh realities of contemporary life and tries to recover the lost Eden of his Edwardian childhood. Both authors believed, with Bertrand Russell, that anyone born after 1914 has never known real happiness. Choosing carefully and covertly, Orwell borrowed and absorbed many elements of Grahame's beast fable (Meyers 2010: 111-112).

HOW ORWELL USED ANTHROPOMORPHISM TO SINISTER EFFECT

Animal allegory is used overtly by Orwell as a vehicle to deliver this political satire, but a comprehensive reading of *Animal Farm* must appreciate the contrast between its allegorical and satirical elements. Distinct from classical fables, in which evil goes punished and good is rewarded, Orwell's tale ends on a negative and cynical note. Orwell also used anthropomorphism in *Animal Farm* to achieve a sinister effect. Whereas many more traditional fairy tales would often feature animals walking on two legs and wearing human clothes, this convention is used by Orwell as a metaphor for social inequality. It is in seeing the pigs at the end of the novel shakily emerging from the farmhouse, clad in human clothes, which turns the other animal's pride into horror (Baker 2001: 151). There is a sense of inevitability to *Animal Farm*'s unsolvable problems.

The animal metaphors, symbolism, similes and allegory that appear throughout Orwell's writings often attempt to articulate a political idea or inspire an emotional response from the reader, through cultural association. However, when we trace back to the Aesopian origins of this form of literary device, we see that the theme Orwell expounded on was decidedly more instructive.

The disparity between the fairy tale theme and political satire comes in the form of tongue-in-cheek humour from the narrating voice. In this way, Orwell uses the expectations of the fairy tale to heighten the impact of the satire it encapsulates:

> The fairy story genre conditions one to certain expectations, an inevitability, a certain and set ethical development of specific issues in which the 'good' get rewarded and the 'bad' punished, according to the terms of the society they are written for (Hunter 1998: 33).

This deliberate divergence from fairy tale convention instils a heightened sense of injustice in the reader, not only from the content of the story, but from the text's failure to produce its anticipated moral message and happy ending. This is in stark contrast to the often didactic roots of animal allegory. Other deviations are also worth noting; while Orwell was to an extent bound by the fairy tale form, *Animal Farm* has none of the fairies, princes, witches, spells or magic transformation associated with the archetypal fairy story (Kirschner 2004: 772). The fairy tale was used as a foundation for Orwell's historical metaphor and political commentary.

Creating satire with farmyard animals leaves an imprint of Orwell's personal interest in nature and his literary influences. However, Orwell implants his own character into *Animal Farm* in a more direct fashion. Characters in Orwell's novels are frequently mirror images of their creator. *Nineteen Eighty-Four*'s hero, Winston Smith, is a projection of Orwell's failing health. The description of Winston as 'a bowed, grey-coloured, skeleton-like thing' (Orwell 2013 [1949]: 271) takes its inspiration from the author's own deathly appearance, when he saw his naked reflection in a sanatorium mirror in 1948, ravaged with tuberculosis and on the brink of death (Bowker 2003).

This presence does not escape *Animal Farm*; Benjamin the donkey has been interpreted as the autobiographical voice of Orwell. Crook explains that Benjamin's 'witty all-knowing cynicism could represent Orwell's personal bitter-sweet experience of the abuse of political power' (Crook 2016). The donkey at one point expresses scepticism, standing out in this regard from the other primarily unquestioning animals. He objects when Boxer the horse is taken away to the knacker's yard:

CHARLIE SALTER

'Quick, quick!' he shouted. 'Come at once! They're taking Boxer away!' Without waiting for orders from the pig, the animals broke off work and raced back to the farm buildings (Orwell 2003 [1945]: 106).

Throughout *Animal Farm*, Orwell's narrative voice presents us with a lot of information the 'lesser' animals are not privy to, and in this respect, this act by Benjamin is an extension of this. As Kirschner explains:

> …Benjamin tells the animals what they cannot 'read' for themselves, *as the author/narrator has been doing for us*. By usurping authorial function, Benjamin suddenly *becomes* the author – not by prudently keeping silent, but by placing sympathy before safety. He becomes 'Orwell' when, through him, the 'author' suddenly seems to drop his mask and show where his heart lies (Kirschner 2004: 765).

The animal metaphors, symbolism, similes and allegory that appear throughout Orwell's writings often attempt to articulate a political idea or inspire an emotional response from the reader, through cultural association. However, when we trace back to the origins of this form of literary device, we see that the theme Orwell expounded on was decidedly more instructive. When studying its roots in literature, one must also consider the Romantic period. Romanticism originated in Europe toward the end of the 18th century, and is often considered to some degree a reaction to the Industrial Revolution. The perspective presented by Romanticist writers and artists often offered a glorified perspective of the past and nature. In this regard, it is easy to draw a comparison to Orwell's writing. A Romanticist approach can be read in the anti-industrialist sentimentality contained in *Coming Up For Air*, and the similar misty-eyed 'back to nature' sensibility of his essay 'Some Thoughts on the Common Toad' (1970b [1946]), in which Orwell implores the reader to retain a love of nature and animals, and to resist blind admiration for the steel and concreate of the modern world.

ORWELL'S KEEN EYE: THE COMMON TOAD AND THE NATURAL WORLD

His *Tribune* column 'Some Thoughts on the Common Toad' (originally published on 12 April 1946) is exemplary in providing an insight into Orwell's 'love of animals, the changing of the seasons and the extraordinarily intense way in which he observed nature' (Keeble 2015: 21). In the column, Orwell was explicit in his justification for his use of such analogies:

> I think that by retaining one's childhood love of such things as trees, fishes, butterflies and – to return to my first instance –

toads, one makes a peaceful and decent future a little more probable, and that by preaching the doctrine that nothing is to be admired except steel and concrete, one merely makes it a little surer that human beings will have no outlet for their surplus energy except in hatred and leader worship (Orwell 1970b [1946]: 175).

Orwell writes with a first-person voice about his passion for nature – his language and choice of analogy provide us with an insight into the political ideologies that we now see as quintessential to 'Orwellian' writing. 'Some Thoughts on the Common Toad' is illustrative of a critical attitude towards socialism, a stance which was prefigured in his *The Road to Wigan Pier* (1937). By voicing his opinions through the life cycle of a toad, Orwell communicates a scepticism of a form of socialism based on the worship of machines and technology.

These ideas would go on to feed into the harsh urban dystopia featured in *Nineteen Eighty-Four* (Marks 2011: 163). Symbolically, foreshadowed by his dreams of the 'Golden Country', *Nineteen Eighty-Four*'s protagonist, Winston Smith, first experiences his sexual awakening in the country side. Once again, Orwell turns to the majesty of nature to deliver his message. In a passage reverberating of the fish in *Coming Up For Air* he writes of an idyllic pool where huge fish wave their tails. In *Nineteen Eighty-Four*, the lovers also observe a singing thrush, which is described in great detail, serving as a metaphor for the pleasure of attaining freedom (Orwell 2013 [1949]: 123).

Much like in 'Some Thoughts on the Common Toad', his essay 'A Good Word for the Vicar of Bray' (1970c [1946]) shows us an Orwell who championed nature as a symbol for all that is good in the world. Starting with derisive descriptions of the vicar and some other seedy characters, the piece then shifts its focus to the vicar's act of planting a yew tree in his churchyard. Orwell derived great significance from this act and, once again, an argument was made for the unifying power of nature and its intrinsic link to personal and positive thoughts (Marks 2011: 164).

These essays give us an insight into the motives behind Orwell's future use of allegory and anthropomorphism. Through these essays, animals and nature become the basis for his political views, and, as Marks explains, a case is made by Orwell that 'the love of nature is not sentimental but has vital political implications' (ibid: 162). These pieces – examples of regular essays he wrote for the socialist newspaper *Tribune* – allowed Orwell not only to comment on politics, but also express his fascination with the changing seasons and wildlife. This interest was heralded in *Homage to Catalonia* (2013 [1938]), in which Orwell often described his experience in the Spanish Civil War from an unconventional angle, shifting the focus from human concerns by filling the pages with rich images of the landscape he observed around him:

> The winter barley was a foot high, crimson buds were forming on the cherry trees (the line here ran through deserted orchards and vegetable gardens), and if you searched the ditches you could find violets and a kind of wild hyacinth like a poor specimen of a bluebell. Immediately behind the line there ran a wonderful, green, bubbling stream, the first transparent water I have seen since coming to the front (ibid: 49).

Observations such as these echo his previous attempts to come to terms with the dramatic Indian scenery in *Burmese Days* (2001 [1934]). To what extent Orwell's descriptive language represents the man himself, or some invented persona, is perhaps unclear, but one senses a candid sincerity when he writes about this subject.

If there is any doubt cast on the authenticity at the core of these metaphors, we can gain a further insight into Orwell's attraction to nature in his personal letters. In one sent to his close friend and one-time love interest, Brenda Salkeld, in September 1934, he describes baby hedgehogs managing to get into his house through the French windows:

> The hedgehogs keep coming into the house, and last night we found one in the bathroom: a little tiny hedgehog no bigger than an orange. The only thing I could think was that it was a baby of one of the others, though it was fully formed – I mean, it had prickles (Taylor 2003: 130).

This letter may at first seem unimportant, but taking a retrospective view, its significance arises in a number of ways. The letter is an example of the eye for detail, and love and concern for animals we see in the essays and novels which followed. However, the aspect of the letter that is most revealing is the lamentation that follows the description of the hedgehogs: 'This age makes me so sick that sometimes I am compelled to stop at a corner and start calling down curses from Heaven' (ibid). This passage epitomises the Orwell we are most familiar with and, as Taylor puts it, is a prime example of 'Orwell being Orwell' (ibid). Here, as he would subsequently develop in *Coming Up For Air* and later, 'Some Thoughts on the Common Toad', Orwell voices his sense of malaise with the modern world, using its disparity with nature as a mouthpiece to articulate this outlook.

Previously, Orwell had conversely used nature as a symbol for the *wrongs* of society. In *Keep the Aspidistra Flying* (2000 [1936]), Orwell used the potted aspidistra plant as a representation of the tedious conformity of middle class life. The novel, which tells the story of Gordon Comstock, a failed poet with objections to capitalism, is widely considered to be a largely autobiographical work. Again, this choice of allegory demonstrates Orwell's propensity to return to objects from nature when constructing a story. The choice of the aspidistra plant in particular, is indicative of Orwell's eye for detail. As an unremarkable-appearing, common potted plant, requiring little sunlight to survive, it serves as a carefully selected allegorical device for the sentiment of the novel. Orwell was fond of gardening, and he and his first wife, Eileen, enjoyed planting flower bushes and fruit trees in their cottage garden (Crick 1992 [1982]: 374).

In the spring of 1940, Orwell wrote a short retrospective piece about his life for an American writers' directory. In the piece, he lists the things that matter most to him (first and foremost gardening), and things he dislikes. This extract is revealing of both Orwell's love of a pastoral life, and his aversion to certain aspects of modernity:

> Outside my work the thing I care most about is gardening, especially vegetable gardening. I like English cookery and English beer, French red wines, Spanish white wines, Indian tea, strong tobacco, coal fires, candlelight and comfortable chairs. I dislike big towns, noise, motor cars, the radio, tinned food, central heating and 'modern' furniture (Bowker 2003: 263).

Keep the Aspidistra Flying was not the first time Orwell had written about plants; in his 21 January 1944 'As I Please' column for *Tribune*, he wrote about a large rose bush he was particularly proud of – leading to an irate anonymous reader to write him an 'indignant letter' complaining 'that rose bushes are bourgeois' (Shelden 1991: 269-270).

NATURE VS HUMANITY

Much has been written about the political views which motivated the scathing commentary contained in *Animal Farm*. But Orwell himself claimed his animal fable was inspired by a far more tangible source. In the Ukrainian edition's foreword to *Animal Farm*, he described the revelation that would lead to one of his most seminal novels:

> …the actual details of the story did not come to me for some time until one day (I was then living in a small village) I saw a little boy, perhaps ten years old, driving a huge cart-horse along a narrow path, whipping it whenever it tried to turn. It struck me that if only such animals became aware of their strength we should have no power over them, and that men exploit animals in much the same way as the rich exploit the proletariat. I proceeded to analyse Marx's theory from the animals' point of view. To them it

was clear that the concept of a class struggle between humans was pure illusion, since whenever it was necessary to exploit animals, all humans united against them: the true struggle is between animals and humans (Orwell 2003 [1945]: 97).

This observation would help form the portrayal of humans as oppressive, evil agents in Orwell's farmyard allegory.

Like the animal's failed attempt to construct an electric windmill, a frequent theme running through Orwell's writing is the crisis of the modern age, and the direct opposition that it poses to traditional lifestyles and wholesome values. This theme is often captured in descriptions of the natural world. Orwell's *Coming Up For Air* and his essay, 'Some Thoughts on the Common Toad' both use animals and rurality as a metaphor to emphasise what war and unchecked capitalism threaten. This theme does not elude his last novel. In *Nineteen Eighty-Four*, Winston Smith's recurring dreams of the 'Golden Country' – 'an old, rabbit-bitten pasture, with a foot-track wandering across it and a molehill here and there' (Orwell 2013 [1949]: 30), underpins the notion of a natural world under threat, while also evoking images from Orwell's childhood. As Bowker explains in his Orwell biography: 'In his mind, the crisis of the modern age was epitomised by the way he related to nature as a boy' (Bowker 2003).

Orwell creates visions of utopia by drawing upon an intense nostalgia for his Thames-side Edwardian childhood. This nostalgia underpins much of his writing, but is perhaps most profound in *Nineteen Eighty-Four* and *Coming Up For Air*. Aside from his dreams of the 'Golden Country', *Nineteen Eighty-Four*'s Winston Smith, feels 'a sort of nostalgia, a sort of ancestral memory' (Orwell 2013 [1949]: 97) for the past. Exaggerated by this contrast, Orwell is able to develop a subversive viewpoint – that Airstrip One, the present in which the novel is set – is 'intolerable'. Winston laments: 'Why should one feel it to be intolerable unless one had some kind of ancestral memory that things had once been different?' (Orwell 2013 [1949]: 59-60). Orwell writes as if Winston's 'ancestral memory' is his own. *Coming Up For Air* features its own 'Golden Country', found in George Bowling's memories of Lower Binfield. His pilgrimage back to his hometown is disastrous, leading him to conclude that 'there's no way back to Lower Binfield' (Orwell 2001 [1939]: 237). As Rai puts it: 'The prelapsarian world of which it is a symbol is irretrievably lost' (Rai 1990: 85). Just as the totalitarian nightmare world of *Nineteen Eighty-Four* has destroyed all but a vague memory of the old world.

CONCLUSION

It is difficult to imagine Orwell's writing without the conspicuous inspiration drawn from his fascination with the natural world. Part of Orwell's lasting appeal owes to the imprint of this personality. This personal approach makes audiences connect with his writing, as Rodden puts it: 'Orwell's audiences *care* about him, both as a writer and a man. His literary personality and personal life have exerted a spell on generations of readers' (Rodden 2014: 29). While Orwell is conventionally defined by his political insights, and the depiction of dystopia in *Nineteen Eighty-Four*, it is the tension between nature's beauty and the modern world of dictatorship, bureaucracy and warfare that more consistently defines Orwell.

When we consider Orwell's tendency to return to nature, we gain an insight into a foundational element of his literary voice. This bucolic passion is at the core of many of his works. While many of the natural analogies Orwell uses are an effective tool in expressing his political viewpoints, we should also delve deeper and consider why these images, in particular, were selected. This will provide us with an awareness of how Orwell's writing was, in large part, shaped by harking back to an Edwardian childhood he viewed as idyllic, and a perpetual fascination with the natural world.

REFERENCES

Aesop (1997 [620-564 BCE]) *Aesop's Fables* (illustrated by Jacob Lawrence), Seattle: University of Washington Press

Aguirre, A. (2016) Animal Farm *and the Beast Fable*, British Library. Available online at http://www.bl.uk/20th-century-literature/articles/animal-farm-and-the-beast-fable, accessed on 2 July 2016

Baker, S. (2001) *Picturing the Beast: Animals, Identity, and Representation*, Illinois: The University of Illinois Press

Baker-Smith, D. (1987) *Between Dream and Nature: Essays on Utopia and Dystopia, Vol. 61*, Amsterdam: Rodopi

Boakes, R. (1984) *From Darwin to Behaviourism: Psychology and the Minds of Animals*, Cambridge: Cambridge University Press

Bowker, G. (2003) *George Orwell*, London: Little, Brown

Crick, B. (1992 [1982]) *George Orwell: A Life*, London: Penguin Books

Dickstein, M. (2007) *Animal Farm*: History as fable, Rodden, J (ed.) *The Cambridge Companion to George Orwell*, Cambridge: Cambridge University Press pp 133-145

Fletcher, A. (2012) *Allegory: The Theory of a Symbolic Mode*, Princeton: Princeton University Press

Fudge, E. (2002) *Animal*, London: Reaktion Books Ltd

Hunter, L. (1998) *Animal Farm*: Satire into Allegory, Holderness G. and Loughrey, B. (eds) *New Casebooks: George Orwell: Contemporary Critical Essays*, Hampshire: Macmillan Press Ltd pp 31-46

Keeble, R. L. (2015) 'There is Always Room for One More Custard Pie': Orwell's Humour, Keeble, R. L. and Swick, D. (eds) *Pleasures of the Prose: Journalism and Humour*, Suffolk: Abramis Academic Publishing pp 10-25

Kennedy, J. S. (1992) *The New Anthropomorphism*, Cambridge: Cambridge University Press

Kirschner, P. (2004) The Dual Purpose of *Animal Farm*, *The Review of English Studies, New Series*, Vol. 55, No. 222 pp 759-786

Lefkowitz, J. B. (2014) Aesop and Animal Fable, G. L. Campbell (ed.) *The Oxford Handbook of Animals in Classical Thought and Life*, Oxford: Oxford University Press pp 1-23

Marks, P. (2011) *George Orwell the Essayist: Literature, Politics and the Periodical Culture*, London: Bloomsbury Publishing

Meyers, J. (2000) *Orwell: Wintry Conscience of a Generation*, New York: W. W. Norton and Company

Meyers, J. (2010) *Orwell: Life and Art*, Illinois: University of Illinois Press

Orwell, G. (2001 [1934]) *Burmese Days*, London: Penguin Books

Orwell, G. (2009 [1936]) *Shooting an Elephant: And Other Essays*. London: Penguin Books. *Shooting an Elephant* is available online at https://www.theorwellprize.co.uk/the-orwell-prize/orwell/essays-and-other-works/shooting-an-elephant/, accessed on 1 December 2016

Orwell, G. (2000 [1936]) *Keep the Aspidistra Flying*, London: Penguin Books

Orwell, G. (2013 [1938]) *Homage to Catalonia*, London: Penguin Books

Orwell, G. (2001 [1939]) *Coming Up For Air*, London: Secker and Warburg

Orwell, G. (2003 [1945]) *Animal Farm: A Fairy Story*, London: Penguin Books

Orwell, G. (1970a [1946]) *Politics vs. Literature: An Examination of Gulliver's Travels*, Orwell, S. and Angus, I. (eds) *The Collected Essays, Journalism and Letters: Vol. 4*, London: Penguin pp 241-260

Orwell, G. (1970b [1946] Some Thoughts on a Common Toad, Orwell, S. and Angus, I. (eds) *The Collected Essays, Journalism and Letters: Vol. 4*, London: Penguin pp 171-175

Orwell, G. (1970c [1946]) A Good Word for the Vicar of Bray, Orwell, S. and Angus, I. (eds) *The Collected Essays, Journalism and Letters: Vol. 4*, London: Penguin pp 181-184. First published in *Tribune*, 26 April 1946

Orwell, G. (2004 [1946]) *Why I Write*, London: Penguin Books

Orwell, G. (2013 [1949]) *Nineteen Eighty-Four*, London: Penguin Books

Orwell, G. (2001 [1998]) *Keeping Our Little Corner Clean, 1942-1943*, Davison, Peter (ed.) *Collected Works of George Orwell, Vol. 14*, London: Secker and Warburg

Rai, A. (1990) *Orwell and the Politics of Despair: A Critical Study of the Writings of George Orwell*, Cambridge: Cambridge University Press

Rodden, J. (2003) Appreciating *Animal Farm* in the New Millennium, *Modern Age*, Vol. 45, No. 1 pp 67-76

Rodden, J. (2014) How Orwell Became 'A FAMOUS AUTHOR', *Midwest Quarterly*, Vol. 56, No. 1 pp 26-45

Shelden, M. (1991) *Orwell: The Authorised Biography*, London: Heinemann

Taylor, D. J. (2003) *Orwell: The Life*, London: Chatto and Windus

NOTE ON THE CONTRIBUTOR

Charlie Salter studied Film Production at the University for the Creative Arts, Farnham. He went on to complete a Master's Degree in Arts Journalism at Lincoln University, and his final dissertation was on George Orwell.

PAPER

C. L. R. James, George Orwell and 'Literary Trotskyism'

CHRISTIAN HØGSBJERG

This paper will examine the little discussed relationship of George Orwell with the black Trinidadian Marxist and Pan-Africanist C. L. R. James. C. L. R. James, together with his boyhood friend and compatriot George Padmore – both radical journalists – are arguably 'missing men from Orwell scholarship'. It will suggest that through considering what John Newsinger called Orwell's 'literary Trotskyism' we can understand the importance of Orwell's relationship to James, a leading figure in the early British Trotskyist movement. This paper will further explore parallels in the life and work of James and Orwell with respect to the importance of the British Empire in their early intellectual formation, their actual short-lived relationship as anti-Stalinist socialist intellectuals once they met after Orwell's return from fighting in Spain, and James's later reflections on Orwell. This paper will hopefully also illuminate some of the critical, wider complexities of Orwell's relationship to the African diaspora..

Keywords: C. L. R. James, George Padmore, Africa, Trotskyism, Empire

INTRODUCTION

In *Orwell and Marxism: The Political and Cultural Thinking of George Orwell*, Philip Bounds situates Orwell as a writer in the 1930s in relationship to 'the young literary intellectuals who were either members of, or closely associated with, the Communist Party of Great Britain (C. P. G. B.) in the 1930s and 1940s' (2009: 2). But for all the general power and persuasion of his argument with respect to these writers, Bounds does not mention even in passing another critical 'young literary, Marxist intellectual' whom Orwell knew during this period: the black Trinidadian C. L. R. James, a leading figure of the early British Trotskyist movement.

James had made a name for himself in colonial Trinidad as a writer of short stories and after moving to Britain in 1932 published the pioneering West Indian novel *Minty Alley* (1936). In Britain, James wrote a play about the heroic leader of the Haitian Revolution, *Toussaint Louverture* (1934), which was performed on the West

CHRISTIAN HØGSBJERG

End stage in 1936 with Paul Robeson in the title role, and author of two path-breaking works of historical literature, *World Revolution: The Rise and Fall of the Communist International* (1937) and *The Black Jacobins: Toussaint Louverture and the Haitian Revolution* (1938) (see Høgsbjerg, 2014).

Yet in excluding James from a consideration of the question of 'Orwell and Marxism', Bounds is not alone, for James – and to a lesser extent, George Padmore, James's boyhood friend and compatriot and another Marxist and anti-colonialist journalist active in Britain during the 1930s and 1940s, whom Orwell helped publish in *Tribune* during the 1940s (see Hooker 1967: 71) – are perhaps some of the most notable 'missing men' in Orwell scholarship.[1] My hopes that this general neglect would be overcome were raised when I saw that the index to the *Cambridge Companion to George Orwell* had 'James, C.' listed in the index. However, on closer inspection this turned out to be, in fact, a reference to the critic Clive James (2007: 126). As this paper will hopefully suggest, James did deserve to be registered in such a volume at least somewhere and, indeed, the relationship between James and Orwell deserves much closer attention than it has received to date.

This is not to say that James has been completely absent from Orwell scholarship, thanks mainly to writers on Orwell coming from the Trotskyist, and especially from the International Socialist (I. S.) tradition founded by the Palestinian Trotskyist Tony Cliff, whose Marxist analysis of the Soviet Union as 'state capitalist' and general stress on 'socialism-from-below' was if not identical at least broadly comparable to that of James (see Callinicos 1990: 73-79). The pioneering analysis of Orwell coming from a writer from the I. S. tradition was a 1969 article in *International Socialism* by Peter Sedgwick, an important early translator of Victor Serge, entitled simply 'George Orwell: International Socialist?' Thirty years later, in 1999, John Newsinger in *Orwell's Politics* produced the most significant piece of Orwell scholarship in the spirit of Sedgwick and the I. S. tradition. Newsinger discusses James in the context of Orwell's views of Rudyard Kipling as a writer, noting the positions of both James and Orwell on Kipling were loosely comparable (1999: 11). He also introduces the critical idea of Orwell as a 'literary Trotskyist', a framework without which it is arguably impossible to begin to make sense of the political importance of someone such as James for Orwell. Christopher Hitchens – a one-time member of the International Socialists – has also commented astutely, if briefly, on the relationship of James and Orwell as writers in, for example, *Orwell's Victory* where he notes that 'the edifice' of Orwell's work, though 'so much identified with sturdy English virtues, owes a great deal to the unspoken international of persecuted oppositionists who withstood "the midnight of the century" – the clasping of hands between Hitler and Stalin' (2003: 57-58). He continues:

In Orwell's letters and journalism one finds knowing and educated references to Victor Serge ... to C. L. R. James, the Trinidadian literary genius who wrote *Black Jacobins*, a history of Toussaint L'Ouverture's revolution in Haiti, then quarrelled memorably with the Comintern, and wrote the best book ever published on the ethics and history of cricket [*Beyond a Boundary*, 1963] ... to Boris Souvarine ...there may be a sort of literary-political alchemy or chemistry which ensures that the right critic notices the right book, or that the right intellectuals and hard cases come into contact with one another (ibid).

Paul Foot, who – like Hitchens – had known James personally, situated Orwell a little more broadly, alongside 'contemporary writers who, as did Orwell, rejected Stalinism without ever ingratiating themselves with the authorities: C. L. R. James, Richard Wright, Arthur Koestler' (Foot 2000: 93). Foot was here possibly too kind to Orwell, almost certainly too kind to Wright, and without a doubt way too kind to Koestler – but nonetheless, what marks particularly figures such as Wright, Koestler, James and Orwell (and, for that matter, Victor Serge and Boris Souvarine) out from the bulk of other left-wing thinkers of their generation was the eloquence with which they indicted not simply the injustices and inequality of capitalism and the horrors of fascism, but also the most powerful force arguing for 'socialism' – Stalinism.[2]

Their mercilessly critical approach to propaganda which covered up the crimes of the Soviet Union, so far out of line with what was fashionable or even deemed 'acceptable' in conventional left-wing discourse at the time, has to be understood if we are to consider their significance as writers. Indeed, both Koestler, the author of *Darkness at Noon* (1940), and Orwell became seen in the West as models of integrity and examples of ideal 'public intellectuals' for their opposition to the 'totalitarianism' not just of the far-right but also of that of Stalinist Russia. As the opening shots of the Cold War took place, Koestler swung behind 'the West' and allowed his work to be used as an ideological weapon against 'communism'. Orwell never succumbed to liberal anti-communism, but his illness and profound isolation towards the end of his life meant that he tragically did not resist such an interpretation of his work with the energy and vigour with which he might have done. The writings of Koestler and Orwell accordingly became widely republished and part of the set reading in schools in Britain and America. James very occasionally veered close towards anti-communism in his writings on 'totalitarianism' during the early 1950s (see for example 'A Natural and Necessary Conclusion' in his 1953 work of literary criticism on *Moby Dick*, *Mariners, Renegades and Castaways: Herman Melville and the World We Live In*). Yet unlike Koestler, and for that matter even Wright and to some degree Orwell himself, James nonetheless stood out as someone who always refused to

CHRISTIAN HØGSBJERG

compromise with imperialism and state power – and, accordingly, as a lifelong revolutionary socialist remained marginalised for almost all his life.

If it is this personal marginalisation of James during his own lifetime which most clearly explains why he has also been somewhat neglected within Orwell scholarship, one might also detect a more general silence with respect to the critical but clearly complex relationship of Orwell to Africa, Africans and people of African descent. The question of Orwell and Empire in general has obviously long been a critical reference point given his formation as a colonial policeman and longstanding relationship to Burma, India and South Asia in general. And there is rightly renewed interest in Orwell's thinking on questions of race and racism (see Stewart 2004) and his relationship to figures like the Indian writer and radical Mulk Raj Anand (see Nasta 2011). Newsinger, for example, in his *The Blood Never Died: A People's History of the British Empire*, notes Orwell's description of imperialism in *Burmese Days* as 'the policeman and the soldier holding the "native" down, while the businessman went through his pockets' (2006: 8).

Yet when it comes to discussing Orwell and Africa and the Caribbean, and Africans (such as Jomo Kenyatta) and people of African descent whether African Americans (for instance, Paul Robeson) and Afro-Caribbeans (not only James and Padmore, but also the Jamaican writer Una Marson, whom Orwell worked alongside at the BBC during the war), a kind of 'silencing' again too often takes place. There are positive signs, however, that matters are slowly changing here (for example, Stewart 2004), and Orwell's travel writings about Morocco ('Marrakech') and his *Morocco Diary* (1938-1939) deserve further critical attention from scholars. Perhaps the most remarkable intervention Orwell made in relationship to Africa and the African diaspora came in his famous 1939 essay denouncing British imperialism, 'Not Counting Niggers'. 'What we always forget,' Orwell wrote, 'is that the overwhelming bulk of the British proletariat does not live in Britain, but in Asia and Africa.'[3] This essay will suggest that such relative clarity from Orwell – compared to the overwhelming bulk of the British left – on this question owes a great deal not only to Orwell's experiences of being part of the apparatus of British colonial oppression in Burma (1922-1927) but also the impact made by the anti-colonialist writings and Pan-Africanist activism of figures like James and Padmore.

PARALLELS IN LIVES SHAPED BY EMPIRE AND THE LEGACIES OF COLONIAL SLAVERY

In 2013, when University College London's Legacies of British Slave-ownership project announced that on 30 November 1835, the trustees of George Orwell's Scottish great-great-grandfather, Charles Blair (1743-1820), received £4,442 (equal to roughly £3 million today) as compensation for the 218 formerly enslaved people on the family's East Prospect estate, at St Thomas-in-the-East in Jamaica, it made headlines.[4] In a sense, though, it was not news as such, for as Bernard Crick had noted back in 1980, Charles Blair 'had been a rich man, an owner of plantations and slaves in Jamaica, who had married into the aristocracy; but his fortune had dwindled away by the time his tenth and last son was born'. So Orwell's grandfather 'though a godson and cousin of the Earl of Westmoreland, was under the disagreeable obligation of having, as that last child, to earn his living' (Crick 1980: 6). While it seems that the money inherited from the barbaric bondage of slavery had run out by the time Orwell's father, Richard Blair, 'had to fend for himself from the age of 18' (ibid), becoming a colonial agent in the opium department of the government of Bengal, the contrast between the slave-owning ancestors of Orwell and the enslaved ancestors of C. L. R. James in the British Caribbean are striking. It is not known how much Orwell was aware of his slave-owning family background when he placed his powerful evocation of the barbarism of 'slavery' at the heart of one of the most indelible impressions of totalitarianism in world literature: 'Freedom is Slavery' in *Nineteen Eighty-Four*.

PAPER

Even in novels such as *Nineteen Eighty-Four*, Orwell never totally abandoned all hope in political action and socialism in particular and, as a result, James never included Orwell among his list of intellectuals like Koestler who, he felt, would completely give in to hopelessness and pessimistic despair. Indeed, in a 1964 lecture, James paid tribute to Orwell with these words: '… he became a policeman in Burma and after he had seen the colonial world in Burma, he came back to become the finest, most original journalist in England' (1984: 147-148). Here, the former black colonial subject James put his finger on one key reason why Orwell was able to relate imaginatively to what it felt like to be a victim of 'totalitarianism' – his experience of the British Empire and colonial rule. And though Orwell experienced 'the colonial world' during the 1920s from the perspective of one doing the oppressing (rather than, like James, as one of the oppressed though emerging nationalist whose first book was about the charismatic leader of the Trinidadian Workingmen's Association, *The Life of Captain Cipriani: An Account of British Government in the West Indies*, 1932), it engendered within Orwell a hatred of not just the brutality and hypocrisy of imperialism but also of the dangers of unaccountable state power and rapacious power in general.

Born at the start of the twentieth century in a territory that was part of the British Empire (Bengal), George Orwell (then Eric Blair) grew up in a middle-class family desperate to maintain their position of 'respectability', went to a highly prestigious private school (Eton) during the First World War, received a solid traditional

CHRISTIAN HØGSBJERG

British 'imperialist' education but refused to live up to academic expectations, and get a scholarship to university. All of this was also true of C. L. R. James, born into the emerging black middle-class of colonial Trinidad two years before Orwell in 1901, and who (coached by his schoolteacher father) won a scholarship to attend the prestigious Queen's Royal College in Port of Spain, a school composed overwhelmingly of children of the white colonial elite in Trinidad. Again like James, Orwell developed a great love of English literature (Thackeray and Shakespeare, in particular) from a young age, and after leaving school both aspired to be novelists while also working as journalists and teaching in secondary schools for periods. The close attention both paid to the lives of the working poor and those 'down and out' in colonial Trinidad in the case of James (who moved to Britain in 1932 to try to make his career as a writer), and in Britain and France in the case of Orwell, led towards a distinct sympathy for and later identification with the oppressed and exploited.

As a writer, Derek Walcott once compared James's elegant and graceful prose to not only that of other West Indian writers such as V. S. Naipaul, but also to Nabokov and Orwell (1995: 36). As David Renton has written of the middle-class Haynes, the protagonist of James's novel *Minty Alley* (1936), set in the 'barrack-yards' of Port of Spain:

> British readers would do well to imagine the George Bowling of Orwell's *Coming Up for Air* [1939], transplanted to the Caribbean, optimistic rather than downbeat, but compelled in the same away to maintain a precarious social standing. The story of the book is of Haynes's conversion from onlooker to participant in the lives of his poorer neighbours. All vitality is in the yard (2007: 76-77).

POLITICAL RADICALISATION AMIDST THE GREAT DEPRESSION AND THE RISE OF FASCISM

Both Orwell and James, like many intellectuals of their generation, radicalised politically as a result of living in Britain during the 1930s in the context of the Great Depression and sojourns in continental Europe amidst the rise of fascism. For both these travellers of the British Empire, visits to the depression-hit North of England during this decade and meetings with local militant socialist workers were to be transformative. In the case of James, a ten-month stay (with his compatriot, the outstanding professional cricketer Learie Constantine) in Nelson in north-east Lancashire during 1932-33 was critical for his intellectual and political evolution. In 'Red Nelson', as it was known locally, James witnessed not only poverty, mass unemployment and suffering but also socialist traditions of solidarity emerge in the face of austerity, and a collectivist spirit embodied among a militant working class community of cotton textile weavers taking mass strike action in September 1932 (see James 1969: 120-129; Høgsbjerg 2014: 38-64). It was from his discussions with such militants that James learnt, as he put it in 1936, that 'British imperialism does not govern only the colonies in its own interests ... it governs the British people in its own interests also' (quoted in Høgsbjerg 2014: 206). Masashi Hoshino has usefully contrasted James's radicalisation in the North with that of Orwell, who discovered the English working class while researching what became *The Road to Wigan Pier*, where he declared them to be 'symbolic victims of injustice, playing the same part in England as the Burmese played in Burma ... here in England, down under one's feet, were the submerged working class, suffering miseries which in their different way were as bad as any oriental ever knows' (2001 [1937]: 138).[5]

Both also saw in practice the potential of workers' power to block the advance of fascism in continental Europe. In the case of James, it was after witnessing a mass united working-class mobilisation on the streets of Paris in early 1934 which blocked an attempt of fascists to follow Hitler's victory a year earlier. For Orwell, it came in revolutionary Catalonia while fighting with the Workers' Party of Marxist Unification of Spain (P. O. U. M.) militia (1936-1937). After the thrill of experiencing 'the working class in the saddle' in revolutionary Barcelona, Orwell wrote: 'I have seen wonderful things and at last really believe in Socialism' (quoted in Crick 1980: 214). In 1942, in 'Looking back on the Spanish War', Orwell wrote (1980 [1942]: 603):

> ... the working class will go on struggling against Fascism after the others have caved in. ... They must do, because in their own bodies they always discover that the promises of Fascism cannot be fulfilled. To win over the working class, the Fascists would have to raise the general standard of living, which they are unable and probably unwilling to do. The struggle of the working class is like the growth of a plant. The plant is blind and stupid, but it knows enough to keep pushing towards the light, and it will do this in the face of endless discouragements.

As Peter Sedgwick put it,

> In Orwell's notes upon the British working-class community in the mid-1930s, we have the naturalist's fascinated, microscopic discovery of 'the growth of the plant', of the secret underlife of living cells in motion, 'pushing towards the light'. Without a vision trained to sense these tiny, molecular stirrings, the bursting of Spain's red flower, in the fullness of proletarian insurrection, might well have eluded him. Others were there, after all, and did not notice it (2005:18-19).

After taking a fascist bullet in the throat and witnessing Stalinist counter-revolutionary practices, Orwell's experience in Spain was to be critical and as he famously put it in 1946, in 'Why I Write', the Spanish Civil War 'turned the scale and thereafter I knew where I stood. Every line I have written since ... has been written directly or indirectly against totalitarianism and for democratic socialism' (quoted in Crick 1980: 193). Indeed, as Orwell noted in June 1938, when he decided to join the sister party of the P. O. U. M. after his return to Britain – the Independent Labour Party – 'at a moment like the present', a period of exceptional urgency, 'writing books is not enough. The tempo of events is quickening; the dangers which once seemed a generation distant are staring us in the face. One has got to be actively a Socialist' (1998b [1938]: 384).

As mentioned, James's critical experience politically along the same dramatic lines had come in 1934 while in France, after witnessing a victorious mass display of working class unity on the streets of Paris against the threat of fascism. On the night of 10 February 1934, James later described how he witnessed 'fierce fighting' and 'men were killed ... The proletariat, the stock of 1789 and the 10th August, 1792, of 1830, of 1848 and 1871, came out in their thousands, whether Socialist or Communist' (1994 [1937]: 381). On 12 February 1934, the main union federation, the General Confederation of Labour (C. G. T.), called for a General Strike and at the last minute the French Communist Party called for a demonstration, albeit separately to the main Socialist Party/C. G. T. one. However, instead of the two demonstrations showing their traditional animosity toward each other, on meeting workers spontaneously and gloriously came together to sing anti-fascist slogans. As James wrote, 'it was in the streets that French parliamentarism was saved. The coup had failed' (ibid). Convinced about Trotsky's call for United Front activity to fight fascism, James decided to become an organised Marxist revolutionary himself in the tiny Trotskyist movement on his return to Britain. As he wrote in 1944 in a private letter: '... ten years ago something came into my life and altered its whole course. Everything previous seemed only preparation' (quoted in Grimshaw 1990: 136). Moving from liberal humanism in colonial Trinidad to an intellectual identification with revolutionary socialism after reading Leon Trotsky's *History of the Russian Revolution* (1932) while up in Nelson, James now threw himself into the struggle to change the world. 'I had plunged into a river from which I was never to emerge,' he later recalled (quoted in Høgsbjerg 2014: 66). As a member of the 'Marxist Group' (which was inside the Independent Labour Party from 1934-36) James had seriously considered volunteering to fight in Spain, which he would have done presumably as part of the I. L. P. contingent (he had been chair of Finchley I. L. P.), just as he had planned to go and fight in Ethiopia against Mussolini's Italian forces, but he respected the discipline of the Trotskyist movement which needed him in Britain (see Høgsbjerg 2016).

George Orwell later recalled the appeal of anti-fascism among intellectuals in England, noting:

> ... as early as 1934 or 1935 it was considered eccentric in literary circles not to be more or less 'left'. Between 1935 and 1939 the Communist Party had an almost irresistible fascination for any writer under forty ... for about three years, in fact, the central stream of English literature was more or less directly under Communist control (1989b [1940]: 32).

Orwell here over-states the intellectual allure and organising power of the C. P. G. B. as it attempted to construct a 'Popular Front' against fascism. Yet, as writers and journalists (James wrote on cricket for the *Manchester Guardian* and then the *Glasgow Herald* during the 1930s) on the left who were establishing literary reputations for themselves in Britain, but were not part of the stream of literature associated with writers in the C. P. G. B. analysed by Philip Bounds, it was inevitable that the paths of James and Orwell would cross at some point. And that point came in 1937, soon after Orwell's return from Spain.

WHEN ORWELL READ AND THEN MET JAMES

In April 1937, James had published his pioneering anti-Stalinist history of 'the rise and fall of the Communist International', *World Revolution, 1917-1936* with the independent left-wing publishers Secker and Warburg. James had concluded the work with 'the Spanish Revolution':

> Bourgeois democracy is doomed in Spain. ... the choice lies between the capitalist Fascist dictatorship, or the Socialist Workers' State. If the workers are to win against Franco and his German and Italian allies ... the war must be a revolutionary war by workers and peasants organised in Soviets or other workers' organisations. But the Soviet bureaucracy made the fight for a democratic Spain a condition of assistance; and the bureaucracy and its agents, though active against Franco, are now preventing Spanish workers and peasants from doing the very things that created Soviet Russia (1994 [1937]: 406).

Indeed, James had predicted that 'the day is near when the Stalinists will join reactionary governments in shooting revolutionary workers. They cannot avoid it' (ibid: 389). In May 1937, a month after *World Revolution* had come out, James was tragically proven right as the Republican government with communist support (as witnessed by Orwell) repressed the P. O. U. M. and anarchists in Barcelona by force, imprisoning thousands and murdering dozens. James was, therefore, an obvious person to be asked by his publisher Fredric Warburg to write an introduction for *Red Spanish Notebook*, an account of revolutionary Spain through the eyes of two surrealist poets who had gone to fight for the P. O. U. M. but had left in February 1937, Mary Low and the Cuban Trotskyist Juan Breá. In his introduction to *Red Spanish Notebook*, which came out later in 1937, James praised Low and Breá's achievement as having provided to the ordinary reader, 'better than all the spate of books on Spain, some idea of the new society that is struggling so desperately to be born' as 'worker's power emerged half-way from books' and became 'a concrete alternative to the old slavery' (1937: v-vii).

Orwell, who had just returned wounded from Spain having 'touched and seen' both workers' power and then Stalinist counter-revolutionary terror in Barcelona, reviewed *Red Spanish Notebook* in *Time and Tide* on 9 October 1937, praising the way in which 'by a series of intimate day-to-day pictures ... it shows you what human beings are like when they are trying to behave as human beings and not as cogs in the capitalist machine' (quoted in Davison 1998: 87). Indeed, on returning to London it seems Orwell had picked up a copy of James's *World Revolution*, and on 8 July 1937 had made inquiries as to how many copies it had sold, noting that 'the people who read that book would be the kind likely to read a book on Spain written from the non-Communist standpoint' (quoted in ibid: 38). According to James's comrade Louise Cripps, Orwell, presumably while working on what would become his classic *Homage to Catalonia* in the summer of 1937, visited James and was a 'serious enquirer' into Trotskyism. 'Since he was so vehemently against Stalin's regime in the Soviet Union, he read and approved the literature we had' (1997: 21). Indeed, in his review of *Red Spanish Notebook*, Orwell had noted that 'Mr. C. L. R. James, author of that very able book *World Revolution*, contributes an introduction' (ibid: 87).

The experience of witnessing the counter-revolutionary role played by the Soviet Union and its agents in Spain led both Breá and Orwell to speculate about the nature of the Soviet Union itself. As Breá wondered in the conclusions to *Red Spanish Notebook*, 'let us suppose that Russia is no longer a proletarian state but is making her first steps towards capitalism' (1937: 254-255). Orwell, in *Homage to Catalonia* (1938) – also published by Secker and Warburg – described the 'socialism in one country' being built in Russia by Stalin as little more than 'a planned state-capitalism with the grab-motive left intact' (1989a [1938]: 83).[6] As James later recalled, he thought *Homage to Catalonia* 'a very fine book and it's typical of Orwell: Orwell went and he saw that the Stalinists had ruined the revolution and he wrote it' (quoted in Ramchand 1980: 90). Coming in the midst of Stalin's Great Terror, the Spanish Civil War was to be of critical importance for the political evolution of James, who had already begun to shift from the orthodox Trotskyist position that the Soviet Union was a 'degenerated workers' state' towards an openness towards the possibilities the

Soviet Union under Stalin was now a state capitalist regime. James's key intellectual collaborator during the 1940s, Raya Dunayevskaya, with whom he later formed the 'State-Capitalist Tendency' (later the 'Johnson-Forest Tendency') within American Trotskyism also developed a similar critical approach to the Soviet Union.[7]

During 1937 and 1938 then, both James – who would follow up *World Revolution* with his classic history of the Haitian Revolution, *The Black Jacobins* in 1938 – and Orwell were part of a circle of left-wing writers who gravitated around the publisher Fredric Warburg. As Newsinger notes, Warburg's 'was an embattled firm that was slowly having the life squeezed out of it by the communists for publishing books by the dissident left, by socialists hostile to communism … James's *World Revolution*, Reg Groves's *We Shall Rise Again*, Boris Souvarine's *Stalin*, and André Gide's *Back from the USSR* as well as *Homage to Catalonia*' (1999: 56). Warburg also recalled that most of the 'promising writers' he published were in or around the Independent Labour Party, and included I. L. P. leading figure Fenner Brockway who had been instrumental in making the initial link with Warburg, but also 'Reginald Reynolds. C. L. R. James, George Padmore, Jennie Lee (Aneurin Bevan's wife), Edward Conze, Jomo Kenyatta, Ethel Mannin and George Orwell' (1959: 206). In an interview with Kenneth Ramchand in San Fernando, Trinidad, in September 1980, James recalled: 'I used to meet [Orwell] at Warburg's house', at parties hosted by Fredric Warburg and his wife Pamela de Bayou. Orwell was one of Warburg's important writers and Mr. and Mrs Warburg would give a party and Orwell would come, now I remember those parties very well … standing in a corner, very handsome, very reserved, but having nothing to say was George Orwell…' (quoted in Ramchand 1980: 90).

THE ROAD TO *SOCIALISM AND WAR*

Meeting the author of *World Revolution* could only have helped Orwell clarify his political thinking about British imperialism, Stalinism and the perils of the Communist International's strategy of the 'Popular Front'. As an activist around and then inside the Independent Labour Party, Orwell picked up something of the anti-colonial and Pan-Africanist activism of James (in partnership with figures such as Amy Ashwood Garvey, Padmore and Kenyatta in the London-based groups, the International African Friends of Ethiopia and the International African Service Bureau) and would have registered James's writings on black and colonial liberation such as *The Black Jacobins* and *A History of Negro Revolt* (both 1938). Through the I. L. P., Orwell also met George Padmore, who was the organising spirit of the British Pan-Africanist movement, the leader of the International African Service Bureau and author of works such as *How Britain Rules Africa* (1936) and *Africa and World Peace* (1937).

CHRISTIAN HØGSBJERG

As James wrote in *World Revolution*, 'for suppression, evasion and hard lying the documents of the Soviet Union and the Third International today form, along with British colonial propaganda and fascist demagogy, a trilogy which future historians will contemplate with wonder' (1994: 16). In 1937, Orwell (and Koestler) were only just beginning to see the awful truth behind such a statement but, unlike James, had not yet seriously contemplated the profound consequences that flowed from such a truth. Indeed, it is important to remember James's *World Revolution* and *The Black Jacobins* as contributions at least as important to defending the truth in what James in 1938 called 'an age of propaganda' (2001[1938]: 5) as anything written in this period by Orwell and Koestler.

Unfortunately, the anti-imperialist pamphlet Orwell wrote in 1938 entitled *Socialism and War* was lost, and has never come to light (Rosenwald 2004: 112). What we do have from this period which helps illuminate the influence of James and Padmore on Orwell in this period is the essay 'Not Counting Niggers', first published in the *Adelphi* in July 1939, a review of Clarence K. Streit's book, *Union Now*. Orwell noted that 'the huge British and French empires' with 'their six hundred million disenfranchised human beings' were not 'democracies' but 'in essence nothing but mechanisms for exploiting cheap coloured labour':

> Here and there in the book, though not often, there are references to the 'dependencies' of the democratic states. 'Dependencies' means subject races … Except where the tables of statistics bring it out, one would never for a moment guess what *numbers* of human beings are involved. India, for instance, which contains more inhabitants than the whole of the 'fifteen democracies' put together, gets just a page and a half in Mr Streit's book, and that merely to explain that as India is not yet fit for self-government the *status quo* must continue … *all* phrases like 'Peace Bloc', 'Peace Front', etc … imply a tightening-up of the existing structure. The unspoken clause is always 'not counting niggers'. For how can we make a 'firm stand' against Hitler if we are simultaneously weakening ourselves at home? In other words, how can we 'fight Fascism' except by bolstering up a far vaster injustice? For of course it *is* vaster. What we always forget is that the overwhelming bulk of the British proletariat does not live in Britain, but in Asia and Africa. … The downward slide is happening because nearly all the Socialist leaders, when it comes to the pinch, are merely His Majesty's Opposition, and nobody else knows how to mobilize the decency of the English people, which one meets with everywhere when one talks to human beings instead of reading newspapers. Nothing is likely to save us except the emergence within the next two years of a real mass party whose first pledges are to refuse war and to right imperial injustice. But if any such party exists at present, it

is only as a possibility, in a few tiny germs lying here and there in unwatered soil (1998a [1939]).

We also have Orwell's diaries from Morocco and the evocative essay 'Marrakesh', first published in *New Writing* in Christmas 1939:

> As the storks flew northward the Negroes were marching southward – a long, dusty column, infantry, screw-gun batteries and then more infantry, four or five thousand men in all, winding up the road with a clumping of boots and a clatter of iron wheels.
>
> They were Senegalese, the blackest Negroes in Africa, so black that sometimes it is difficult to see whereabouts on their necks the hair begins. Their splendid bodies were hidden in reach-me-down khaki uniforms, their feet squashed into boots that looked like blocks of wood, and every tin hat seemed to be a couple of sizes too small. It was very hot and the men had marched a long way. They slumped under the weight of their packs and the curiously sensitive black faces were glistening with sweat.
>
> As they went past a tall, very young Negro turned and caught my eye. But the look he gave me was not in the least the kind of look you might expect. Not hostile, not contemptuous, not sullen, not even inquisitive. It was the shy, wide-eyed Negro look, which actually is a look of profound respect. I saw how it was. This wretched boy, who is a French citizen and has therefore been dragged from the forest to scrub floors and catch syphilis in garrison towns, actually has feelings of reverence before a white skin. He has been taught that the white race are his masters, and he still believes it (1980 [1939]: 442-443).

WAR AND 'THE BUREAUCRATIC-TOTALITARIAN MONSTER'

By Christmas 1939, Britain was at war – a war that Orwell would critically support while C. L. R. James was now in the United States, having left in autumn 1938 for a six-month lecture tour that became a fifteen-year sojourn. While in the US, James kept abreast of Orwell's writing, as can be seen from a review of Richard Wright's short story *Bright and Morning Star* that he published under the pseudonym 'James M. Fenwick' in the Trotskyist journal *New International* in November 1941:

> Among all the thousands of authors turning out short stories today, Richard Wright is one of the few who stir the depths of one's pity and anger. Wright's stories shoulder their way through the aimless mass of current fiction because he works with a great theme. His tragedies are not the personal tragedies of a white novelist … nor are they the basically personal tragedies of Langston Hughes's Negro Bohemians, in which the race question adds a certain piquancy but does not become the fiery question of all questions that it does in Wright's novels and stories …

CHRISTIAN HØGSBJERG

Writing from London in a recent issue of *The New Republic*, George Orwell notes in the younger English writers 'the absence of any feeling of purpose', and states that there 'seems no chance of any major literary work appearing until the future is more predictable and thinking people have less feeling of helplessness'. Marion O'Donnell, in an anthology of poetry published in *New Directions*, expresses this same feeling of helplessness in American writers with the question: 'What action now means act as a man should?' In these comments Orwell and O'Donnell reflect very well the bankruptcy of bourgeois literature which, confronted with the greatest crisis in world history, has nothing to say (quoted in Young 1999: 153-54).

Though Orwell never visited the US, he took an interest in the black liberation struggle in America nonetheless, reviewing Richard Wright's *Native Son* in 1940, for example (Stewart 2004: 156-157), while his personal pamphlet collection included the 1943 American Socialist Party pamphlet, *Victory's Victims? The Negro's Future* by A. Philip Randolph and Norman Thomas (Newsinger 1999: 90). In 1943-1944, Orwell used his 'As I Please' column in the left Labour journal, *Tribune*, to campaign not only against institutional racism and the 'colour bar' in Britain but also to challenge American racism, helping defend a black American corporal Leroy Henry who, while in Britain, had been charged with rape and sentenced to death by the American military (see Stewart 2004: 154-155; Hooker 1967: 65).

James would not return to Britain until 1953, when he was forced out of McCarthyite America. By this time Orwell had died, so they never had the opportunity for a reunion.[8] Yet James in America would come to share a similar concern with Orwell about what in *Beyond a Boundary* (1963) James would call 'the bureaucratic-totalitarian monster' (1969: 149). Robert A. Hill has suggested that unfinished manuscript – published posthumously as *American Civilization* – which James was working on in early 1950 as he would have heard the news of the author of *Nineteen Eighty-Four* passing – contained an analysis of totalitarianism which 'marks a sort of political and intellectual homage to Orwell from America'. As Hill notes:

> James's statement that 'the close study of the United States will explain most easily to people of Western Europe why totalitarianism arises, the horrible degradation it represents, its terrible cost to society, the certainty of its overthrow' shows an awareness on the part of James of the potential for a European audience for his work. It would thus complement the discussion of totalitarianism that Orwell's work had already done much to help understand … what is novel for this time is James's insight into the disintegrative character of totalitarianism, in the form of the Stalinist system, a prophetic view of its demise

that counterbalances the assessment of its seemingly absolute character. ... The prescient quality of James's analysis ... is perhaps best summed up in his statement: 'These regimes will collapse ultimately. They solve neither economic, social nor psychological problems. They integrate the personality by destroying it altogether. They destroy the very basis of progress in the productivity of labor; the police state is an economic burden and a psychological cancer' (1993: 336).[9]

In 1944, Orwell had written an essay on Arthur Koestler which stressed the importance of his 'foreignness': 'One striking fact about English literature during the present century is the extent to which it has been dominated by foreigners – for example, Conrad, Henry James, Shaw, Joyce, Yeats, Pound and Eliot' (1980 [1944]: 658). This would later be a theme in James's writings and speeches as well. For example, in a speech he gave in February 1964 in Edinburgh to the West Indian Students Association, 'A National Purpose for Caribbean Peoples', James discussed the 'Englishness' of the canon of 'English literature', taking in authors such as Jonathan Swift, James Joyce (though born Irish), Rudyard Kipling and Joseph Conrad (though born Polish). Here James also paused to make reference to – and pay tribute to – Orwell:

> Who is the finest English journalist of the last twenty years? He, it is true, is an Englishman. But wait a bit, I think you know his name. He wrote a book called *The Road to Wigan Pier* but do you remember his name? He also wrote *Homage to Catalonia*. He is the finest English journalist since the war. His name is George Orwell. You know where he came from? They will tell you Orwell went to Eton – that is undoubtedly true – the establishment of the establishment; but after that he became a policeman in Burma and after he had seen the colonial world in Burma, he came back to become the finest, most original journalist in England. You see, you have to come from outside, to be able, when a civilisation is shaking, to see and carry to a conclusion the things that are being developed (1984: 147-148).

In September 1980, James – now almost eighty years old – was again asked about his thoughts on Orwell by the literary scholar Kenneth Ramchand. Of *Animal Farm*, James said: 'I wasn't swept away by the novel that's all I can say ... I believe in his other writing, he's first of all a very honest straightforward man and he was aware of the tremendous dangers that the state-formed organisation runs ...' (quoted in Ramchand 1980: 90).

ACKNOWLEDGEMENTS

I would like to thank the anonymous readers for their constructive comments on this article in draft, as well as David Howell, who supervised my doctoral thesis on C. L. R. James at the University of York, David Goodway for his insightful discussions with me about

Orwell over a number of years, and finally Masashi Hoshino for giving a stimulating paper on James and Orwell at a one-day forum on 'C. L. R. James Today' in January 2015 at Hitotsubashi University, Tokyo, which I had the privilege to listen to. Obviously, I take sole responsibility for the argument in this essay.

NOTES

[1] For example, there is no mention of C. L. R. James in Michael Shelden (1991) *Orwell: The Authorized Biography*, New York: HarperCollins or D. J. Taylor (2003) *Orwell: The Life*, London: Vintage. George Padmore co-signed a letter alongside Orwell and others that was published in *Forward* in February 1946 to try to clear Trotsky's name over his 'alleged association' with the Nazi government, and was also notably one of those 'crypto-communists' Orwell famously listed and gave to the Information Research Department, the newly-formed state propaganda outfit, in 1949. But since Padmore was a former communist who became a leading anti-colonialist, the British state had long been monitoring him

[2] On Wright, and his links to the US State Department, see Schwarz (2016: 40-41). Koestler ended up becoming a Commander of the British Empire, a member of the Conservative Party and an admirer of Margaret Thatcher. See Cesarani 1999: 496, 527

[3] Orwell's 'Not Counting Niggers' was first published in the *Adelphi* in July 1939, and republished as George Orwell (1998a) 'Review of *Union Now* by Clarence K. Streit', in Peter Davison (ed.) (1998) *The Complete Works of George Orwell*, Vol. 11, London: Secker and Warburg

[4] BBC News (2013) George Orwell family among 3,000 slave-owners who received compensation, 27 February. Available online at http://www.bbc.co.uk/news/uk-21586755, accessed on 1 December 2016

[5] Masashi Hoshino, *Through Englishness to World Revolution: C. L. R. James and George Orwell*. Paper given at a one-day forum on 'C. L. R. James Today' at Hitotsubashi University, Tokyo, 11 January 2015. As Hoshino's paper made clear, James's thoughts on 'Englishness' deserve greater attention, and deeper comparative study in relation with Orwell's more famous reflections, than was possible in this paper

[6] As Orwell noted of the Soviet Union in 1939: 'Is it Socialism, or is it a peculiarly vicious form of state capitalism? All the political controversies … for two years past really circle round this question' (quoted in Newsinger 1999: 111)

[7] For more discussion of this, see Høgsbjerg, 2017 (forthcoming)

[8] During the 1950s, C. L. R. James lived at 70 Parliament Hill in Hampstead, London, which by nice coincidence was close to a former residence of Orwell (77 Parliament Hill). I am grateful to Robert A. Hill for this information

[9] Importantly, James noted in his introduction to *American Civilization* that 'in this volume there is an identification of the regimes of Hitlerism and Stalinism under the common name totalitarian. It must be understood that this implies no identity of the regimes. The characterization has been made merely to emphasize the ultimate social consequences of any kind of regime which does not develop along co-operative lines, developing the creative spirit of the mass. Politically speaking the differences between Stalinism and Fascism, particularly on a world scale, are of immense, in fact, of decisive importance' (1993: 39)

REFERENCES

BBC News (2013), George Orwell family among 3,000 slave-owners who received compensation, 27 February. Available online at http://www.bbc.co.uk/news/uk-21586755, accessed on 1 December 2016

Bounds, Philip (2009) *Orwell and Marxism: The Political and Cultural Thinking of George Orwell*, London: I. B. Taurus

Callinicos, Alex (1990) *Trotskyism*, Minneapolis: University of Minnesota Press

Cesarani, David (1999) *Arthur Koestler: The Homeless Mind*, London: Vintage

Crick, Bernard (1980) *George Orwell: A Life*, London: Secker and Warburg

Cripps, Louise (1997) *C. L. R. James: Memories and Commentaries*, London: Cornwall Books

Davison, Peter (ed.) (1998) *The Complete Works of George Orwell*, Vol. 11, London: Secker and Warburg

Foot, Paul (2000) *Articles of Resistance*, London: Bookmarks

Grimshaw, Anna (ed.) (1990) *Special Delivery: The letters of C. L. R. James to Constance Webb, 1939-1948*, Oxford: Blackwell

Hill, Robert A. (1993) Literary Executor's Afterword, James, C. L. R. *American Civilization*, Oxford: Blackwell pp 293-366

Hitchens, Christopher (2003) *Orwell's Victory*, London: Penguin

Høgsbjerg, Christian (2014), *C. L. R. James in Imperial Britain*, Durham, NC: Duke University Press

Høgsbjerg, Christian (2016) 'The Fever and the Fret': C. L. R. James, the Spanish Civil War and the Writing of *The Black Jacobins*, *Critique*, Vol. 44, Nos 1-2 pp 161-177

Høgsbjerg, Christian (2017 forthcoming) Introduction, James, C. L. R. *World Revolution: The Rise and Fall of the Communist International*, Durham, NC: Duke University Press

Hooker, James R. (1967) *Black Revolutionary: George Padmore's Path from Communism to Pan-Africanism*, London: Pall Mall Press

James, C. L. R. (1937) Introduction, Low, Mary and Breá, Juan, *Red Spanish Notebook: The First Six Months of the Revolution and the Civil War*, London: Secker and Warburg

James, C. L. R. (1963) *Beyond a Boundary*, London: Hutchinson

James, C. L. R. (1984) *At the Rendezvous of Victory: Selected Writings*, London: Allison and Busby

James, C. L. R. (1993) *American Civilization*, Oxford: Blackwell

James, C. L. R. (1994 [1937]) *World Revolution 1917-1936: The Rise and Fall of the Communist International*, New Jersey: Humanities Press

James, C. L. R. (2001 [1938]) *The Black Jacobins: Toussaint L'Ouverture and the San Domingo Revolution*, London: Penguin

Low, Mary and Juan Breá (1937) *Red Spanish Notebook: The First Six Months of the Revolution and the Civil War*, London: Secker and Warburg

Nasta, Susheila (2011) Sealing a Friendship: George Orwell and Mulk Raj Anand at the BBC (1941–43), *Wasafari*, Vol. 26, No. 4 pp 14-18

Newsinger, John (1999) *Orwell's Politics*, Basingstoke: Macmillan

Newsinger, John (2006) *The Blood Never Dried: A People's History of the British Empire*, London: Bookmarks

Orwell, George (2001 [1937]) *The Road to Wigan Pier*, London: Penguin

Orwell, George (1989a [1938]) *Homage to Catalonia*, London: Penguin.

George Orwell, (1998b [1938]) Why I Joined the Independent Labour Party, Deane, Patrick (ed.) *History in Our Hands: A Critical Anthology of Writings on Literature, Culture and Politics from the 1930s*, London, Leicester University Press pp 384-385

CHRISTIAN HØGSBJERG

Orwell, George (1998a [1939]) Review of *Union Now* by Clarence K. Streit Davison, Peter (ed.) *The Complete Works of George Orwell*, Vol. 11, London: Secker and Warburg

Orwell, George (1989b [1940]) *Inside the Whale and Other Essays*, London: Penguin

Orwell, George (1980 [1942]) Looking Back on the Spanish Civil War, *Down and Out in Paris and London et al*, London: Secker and Warburg/Octopus pp 595-607

Orwell, George (1980 [1944]) Arthur Koestler *Down and Out in Paris and London et al*, London: Secker and Warburg/Octopus pp 658-664

Ramchand, Kenneth (1980) Interview with C. L. R. James in San Fernando for Banyan, September 1980, unpublished manuscript. Available online http://www.clrjames.uk/wp-content/uploads/2015/10/Interviews-with-C.L.R.-James-by-Ken-Ramchand.pdf, accessed on 9 December 2016

Renton, Dave (2007) *C. L. R. James: Cricket's Philosopher King*, London: Haus

Rodden, John (ed.) (2007) *The Cambridge Companion to George Orwell*, Cambridge: Cambridge University Press

Rosenwald, Lawrence (2004) Orwell, Pacifism, Pacifists, Cushman, Thomas and Rodden, John (eds) *George Orwell: Into the Twenty-First Century*, Boulder: Paradigm pp 111-125

Schwarz, Bill (2016) Black America and the overthrow of the European colonial order: The tragic voice of Richard Wright, Craggs, Ruth and Wintle, Claire (eds) *Cultures of Decolonisation: Transnational Productions and Practices, 1945-70*, Manchester: Manchester University Press pp 29-50

Sedgwick, Peter (2005 [1969]) George Orwell: International Socialist?, Flewers, Paul (ed.) *George Orwell: Enigmatic Socialist*, London: Socialist Platform pp 3-19

Shelden, Michael (1991) *Orwell: The Authorized Biography*, New York: Harper Collins

Stewart, Anthony (2004) Vulgar Nationalism and Insulting Nicknames: George Orwell's Progressive Reflections on Race, Cushman, Thomas and Rodden, John (eds) *George Orwell: Into the Twenty-First Century*, Boulder: Paradigm pp 145-159

Taylor, D. J. (2004) *Orwell: The Life*, London: Vintage

Walcott, Derek (1995) A Tribute to C. L. R. James, Cudjoe, Selwyn R. and Cain, William E. (eds) *C. L. R. James: His Intellectual Legacies*, Amherst: University of Massachusetts pp 34-48

Warburg, Fredric (1959) *An Occupation for Gentlemen*, London: Secker and Warburg

Young, James, D. (1999) *The World of C. L. R. James: His Unfragmented Vision*, Glasgow: Clydeside Press

NOTE ON THE CONTRIBUTOR

Christian Høgsbjerg is a historian who works at Leeds University Centre for African Studies. He is author of *C. L. R. James in Imperial Britain*, editor of *Toussaint Louverture*, James's 1934 play, and *World Revolution*, James's history of the Communist International, and co-editor of *The Black Jacobins Reader* (all titles with Duke University Press). He is also the author of *Chris Braithwaite: Mariner, Renegade and Castaway* and the co-editor of *Celebrating C. L. R. James in Hackney, London* (both titles with Redwords). He is a member of the editorial board of *International Socialism*.

REVIEWS

Orwell's Nose: A Pathological Biography
John Sutherland
Reaktion Books, London, 2016 pp 256
ISBN 978 1 78023 6483

David Lodge is quoted on both the back and front of the jacket of this exhilarating book that *Orwell's Nose* is 'racily readable'. That is absolutely true as in this brief book John Sutherland, the eminent and frighteningly productive literary scholar, has raced through Orwell's biography full of, as he writes himself, 'oblique, self-indulgent angles' (p. 50). Use of 'pathological' in the subtitle suggests that the study is likely to be grimmer than it is in fact. But it is true that it concentrates on Orwell's interest, indeed almost an obsession, with smell.

The study begins with two famous quotations from Orwell, one from *The Road to Wigan Pier* that 'the lower classes smell' and the other, with no source given but presumably from 'Such, Such Were the Joys' about his prep school days: 'I was damned, I had no money, I was weak, I was ugly, I was unpopular, I had a chronic cough, I was cowardly. I smelt' (p. 7). The first was probably true in the England where Orwell grew up. Bathing, frequently a hip bath in the kitchen, was likely to be at best weekly among the 'lower classes'. Orwell did not mix much with such folk before his contacts with British troops in Burma and later when 'down and out in Paris and London'. Looking back on his schooldays, perhaps he was pleased to identify with the lower classes. But the statement was the sort of exaggerations he enjoyed making about himself. His alleged bedwetting and the punishment for it while at prep school might have been drawing upon the experience of another boy. For Orwell it was important to identify with the oppressed.

In many ways this is a zip through Orwell's life. With full credit given, it depends on the various biographies and other readings that are relevant rather than on archival work. After a long Preface discussing Orwell and smell, Sutherland embarks on Orwell's life story, returning to smell in the writings in which it plays a crucial part. There are good and bad smells. Sutherland rather enjoys using four letter words which he feels Orwell would have employed if the conventions of the time permitted it. Hence he contrasts the bad shit smells of the poor found in their housing and in their hospitals and the good shit animal smells on farms. But there are other themes that Sutherland dwells on such as the importance of Etonians in his life, Richard Rees, David Astor and Cyril Connolly. There is also quite a bit about the association of good smells and his quite active sex life. Orwell particularly liked to make love in sweet smelling woods which, of course, reaches its famous apotheosis with Julia in the Golden Country in *Nineteen Eighty-Four*. Sutherland depicts, presumably accurately, Orwell's proclivity to pounce when talking a walk in the woods with a woman. It was that impulse that led to the break-up in his early previously rather idyllic first romance with Jacintha Buddicom.

Sutherland writes vividly about Orwell's love life. Particularly interesting is the relation with Eleanor Jaques when he was living with his parents in Southwold on his return from Burma in the late 1920s. He was sleeping with her at the same time that he was a good friend of her fiancé, Dennis Collings. Sutherland makes the fascinating point, which I don't remember seeing before, that Collings, who was studying anthropology at Cambridge, told Orwell about Malinowski and being a participant-observer. This may well have helped inspire Orwell to go down and out in order to acquire material to write about.

It's rather surprising that Sutherland says nothing about Kay Ekevall with whom he may have had his most extended affair before marriage. He writes powerfully about the marriage with Eileen and what a difficult match it was. He very interestingly argues that she may have had an important influence on the growth of his literary interests as she read English at Oxford and was a contemporary there of Kathleen and Geoffrey Tillotson and Humphry House. But he does not claim that they were particular friends of hers. He seems to accept without question that Eileen had an affair with Georges Kopp, Orwell's commander in Spain, and he is probably correct. By a nice coincidence it is true that Kopp ultimately did marry an Orwell family connection, but not his cousin, as Sutherland states, but rather Eileen's sister-in-law's half-sister!

The author does permit himself a rather pathological ending to his book suggesting that Orwell dying of tuberculous in University College hospital, fearing the debility that would face him should he survive, might have committed suicide. This seems highly unlikely. But John Sutherland seems quite fond of what would appear to be improbable scenarios, having played with the idea in the 24 February 2016 issue of the *Times Literary Supplement* that his Eton teacher, A. S. F. Gow, might have smothered him in the hospital. Gow did visit his old pupil there. But Sutherland also dismisses the idea as 'nonsense'. That speculation is not returned to in this study, although his relation with Gow is discussed. When at Eton Orwell had published a poem that teased Gow for his presumed homosexuality. Gow had also advised Orwell's father that his son certainly should not go on to Oxbridge, leading to Orwell joining as an officer the Burmese police. As a King's Scholar he probably could have achieved a place at Oxford or Cambridge, but he had not done well at Eton. At that time going on to university was not a necessary step in order to have a successful career. Despite apparently not being on good terms with Gow, Orwell on his return from Burma visited him, Gow having achieved his dream of being a Fellow at Trinity College, Cambridge, seeking advice about his future. Gow may have raised the possibility that Orwell should enter the intelligence services, perhaps for the British, perhaps for the Russians.

If I may be permitted something of a personal reaction to this book, I am pleased that the author calls William Abrahams's and my *The Unknown Orwell* (1972) and *Orwell: The Transformation* (1979) 'foundational' (p. 37) as 'early biographical birds' (p. 74). But there are some aspects of our work that he mentions that I would like to comment on, although with the passage of years it is perfectly possible that my own memory is fallible. Our original intention was not necessarily biographical but rather to concentrate on Orwell and the Spanish Civil War. In any case, I don't believe his prohibition of a biography was as absolute as Sutherland suggests. His widow Sonia Orwell in the early 1960s when we began our work did not seem to have much interest in her late husband and in supporting the prohibition. Our cordial meetings at the White Tower restaurant in London were not much concerned with what direction our study might take. Also, his co-literary executor, Richard Rees, Orwell's patron as editor of the *Adelphi*, rather cruelly portrayed as Ravelston in *Keep the Aspidistra Flying*, assured us that Orwell had not meant the restriction all that strongly but that it reflected his belief, of course true, that no biography could be totally accurate. Orwell was originally to be part of our study of several Englishmen who had participated in the Spanish Civil War. That became a separate book, *Journey to the Frontier* (1966), on John Cornford and Julian Bell. (Incidentally, Sutherland makes a highly improbable and, in a way, shocking passing remark that John Cornford might have been shot in the back by his own side because, although a devout communist, he had served with the P. O. U. M. militia before joining the International Brigade.)

When we returned to Orwell in the mid-1960s, Sonia had become much more possessive of him and withdrew her co-operation. Before the break we had with her permission examined what was then in the Orwell archive in University College London and, in fact, had been the means of making some additions to it. We had already spoken to many who had known Orwell, some of whom she had suggested we contact. But in reaction to the publication of our first Orwell book she appointed Bernard Crick as his official biographer. Later on she tried to stop his book but he had an iron-clad permission to publish. In any case, we had never intended to

REVIEW

write a complete biographical study but rather just through his experiences in the Spanish Civil War. Sutherland tends, in my view, not to give that sufficient weight. Spain committed him to the socialist vision because of what he experienced in Barcelona when he arrived there in December 1936. But then the May days in the same city in the following year also demonstrated to him how easily socialism could fail. Hence *Animal Farm* and *Nineteen Eighty-Four*.

John Sutherland goes where he wishes and smell is not the only aspect that is investigated here. One is grateful for the various directions taken in this short book. It is written in an easy and rather off-hand way that at times is a bit disconcerting but is generally insightful and wide-ranging – as if he is having a conversation with his reader. A rather idiosyncratic short commentary on Orwell's life and work, it serves as an excellent introductory text with a particular emphasis on smell.

Peter Stansky,
Stanford University

Dictating to the Mob: The History of the BBC Advisory Committee on Spoken English

Jürg R. Schwyter

Oxford University Press, Oxford, 2016 pp 304

ISBN 978 0 1987 3673 8 (hbk)

Since the relative decline of philology in favour of criticism and theory in the study of English literature within the academy, attention paid to linguistic detail in literary works has also correspondingly suffered. If this is true for the written word, is true *a fortiori* for the spoken: the magisterial edition of Eliot's poetry, edited by Christopher Ricks and Jim McCue (2015), includes notes on how Eliot pronounced certain words in his own reading of his work, but this deeply praiseworthy feature is highly unusual. Symptomatically, though, this information is given in re-spelling rather than the International Phonetic Alphabet or some other more accurate method: the presumption of the modernist scholar's ignorance of phonetics is evident, and probably, alas, justified.

This ignorance is curious not only when we consider poetry, but also when we think of the remarkable sociolinguistic importance accent had and continues to have in Britain – and Shaw's *aperçu* about the impossibility of an Englishman opening his mouth without making another Englishman despise him remains true to the point of cliché. Orwell was another great observer of English-language sociolinguistics, as much of his political criticism of the misuse of language begins with keen, albeit impressionistic, observation. Accent seemed to interest him less, although his own experience involving the importance (or more interestingly *lack* of importance) of one's accent when a tramp should not be discounted. His own voice and pronunciation will have to remain conjectural unless somewhere in the BBC archives a recording of it is one day found. But the very fact that he spoke on the BBC means that Jürg R. Schwyter's new book on the history of the BBC Advisory Committee on Spoken English, a work otherwise likely to be overlooked as of interest to a narrower range of scholars in linguistics only, should be of keen interest to Orwell scholars, as well as those working on literature in Britain in the interwar years more generally.

REVIEW

The committee existed between 1926 and 1939, and its influence continued on into Orwell's period at the BBC and beyond, although as a body it ceased to exist for most practical purposes in 1937. Its members included not only Shaw himself but Robert Bridges, the then-Poet Laureate, David Cecil, Rose Macaulay and I. A. Richards (Virginia Woolf turned the invitation down) (pp 96-97). Had the committee continued on into the 1940s, one may imagine that Orwell would have been an obvious person to approach as a prospective member. Schwyter's book is primarily concerned with offering a history of the committee and its bureaucratic struggles both internal and external. In this, thanks to extensive archival research, he succeeds admirably, and the book should be read by anyone with an interest in the history of the BBC (and inter-war institutions more generally, perhaps, due to its insights into the machinations and muddling involved alongside efficiency and innovation). Equally, it sheds light on an under-investigated attempt at language standardisation, with the introduction giving a useful overview of the issues involved for the non-expert. As for the scholar of literature, this book gives a fascinating glimpse of the arguments over the 'correct' pronunciations of individual words that a presenter such as Orwell would have been expected to follow.

It is here, however, that the book, so rich on institutional history, becomes (curiously enough, as Schwyter is a linguist) rather frustrating. Although Appendix IV reproduces the notes on words discussed for the third edition of *Broadcast English I*, the BBC's published guide, as well as those discussed later (including, therefore, comments from 1926 to 1937), Schwyter does go into details of problematic words such as 'ski' (/ʃiː/ or /skiː/?) and 'margarine' (with /dʒ/ rather than /g/, despite Unilever's entreaties: pp 49-53). But very little detail or analysis is offered of individual words. It would be precisely this that would be of most use to the reader interested in literature and cultural history. We know that 'fascism' was discussed in 1933, with 'fásh-izm' (=/ˈfæʃɪzm̩/, presumably) as the pronunciation given as correct; what is not discussed is what other possibilities there were (p. 243). It would be fascinating to know whether Orwell was first introduced to the word in this form, the usual one today and clearly Italian-based and contemporary but with a 'domesticated' /æ/ rather than the more safely foreign /ɑː/, perhaps, or a more distancing classical pronunciation with /sk/ rather than /ʃ/, as opposed to a truly naturalised /s/. This would potentially open up fascinating avenues of research. However, we are not given details of what other pronunciations were heard at the time; all that we are left with are conjectures of the type that I have just offered.

Equally, given Orwell's famous dictum about the need to avoid foreign phrases (and one, therefore, presumes foreign words, too), the treatment of 'questionnaire' raises interesting issues that also go unanswered. This is now /ˌkwestʃəˈneə/, a fully naturalised form that has evidently lost its Frenchness and foreignness. In his reading of his 'Under Which Lyre' (1946), however, W. H. Auden clearly pronounces it as /ˌkestiːɒˈneə/, a form just as evidently still 'foreign' – the pronunciation of <qu> as /k/ rather than /kw/ being the most obvious indicator possible that for the poet at least the word had yet to become one that Orwell would have allowed into his ideal prose. What, though, is the evidence from Schwyter's book and the BBC Advisory Committee on Spoken English? The recommended pronunciation, discussed in July 1930 and September 1934, is given as '**kwestiŏnnáire**' (=/ˌkwestiːɒˈneə/, presumably), which is to say a form half-way between Auden's and the usual modern one (pp 251-252). In other words, the term would appear to have been more naturalised in general use than Auden's later pronunciation would suggest. This conclusion, however, is complicated by the note appended in 1930 – 'Recommended the use of the *English* word "questionary"' (my italics) – which suggests that notwithstanding the suggested Anglicised pronunciation, it was still seen as a foreign import. But then the recommended omission of the 1930 note in 1934 suggests increasing acceptance, *pace* Auden. The conclusion can only be, perhaps unsurprisingly, that 'questionnaire' was in flux through the 1930s: the degree to which such a case study makes our reading of Orwell's fifth rule less simple to judge and apply historically should be clear.

Of course, such questions, fascinating as they be, and as much as they may suggest new approaches for collaboration between those working on language and those working on literature, are not those that Schwyter sets himself to answer. Neither is it his task to explore the ramifications in studies of Orwell's thinking on language and the creation of Newspeak that his unearthing of the

Sub-Committee on Words of 1935-1937 (pp 129-147) may have. This body was created to invent new words for new concepts – had it had its way, we might be talking about 'view-boxes' rather than 'television sets' and 'stop-and-goes' rather than 'traffic lights' (p. 139). If Orwell knew about the sub-committee and its work, then this case of a semi-political bureaucratic body attempting to control vocabulary creation would become a very obvious contender for the source of Newspeak. In this sense, Schwyter's book, aimed as it is at linguists, performs for literary scholars perhaps the most valuable service that a monograph can: it raises questions and suggests new lines of research, besides being an excellent sourcebook for material that would otherwise be buried in archives.

The volume is marred, however, by extremely careless editing. It is worrying that a linguistics text published by OUP should show such an array of errors in printing the International Phonetic Alphabet. For example, the length mark is usually given as a colon, and <ɘ> is mistakenly used on occasion for the shwa (e.g. p. xi). This carelessness sometimes creates wider problems. For instance, when discussing *Broadcast English II*, the 1930 BBC booklet on place-name pronunciation, Schwyter gives as a typical entry that for Wrangaton in Devon. The 1930 BBC IPA is given as <'ræn̩ətən>, which is quite impossible: presumably <n̩> is an error for <ŋ> (p. 124). In a book more carefully edited, either this error would not be there, or, if it was, we could be sure that it was an error from the BBC in 1930. As *Dictating to the Mob* stands, however, we can seldom be sure when and where error has crept in. This, coupled with very poor image reproduction (and the unattractive, jarring and distracting use of a sans-serif typeface for all long quotations), is much to the volume's detriment.

REVIEW

These considerations apart, *Dictating to the Mob*, notwithstanding its ostensibly niche (whether /niːʃ/ or /nɪtʃ/ appears not to have been discussed) subject matter, is a work that can be read with great interest by those working on Orwell, and on interwar British culture more generally, who would normally never consider language standardisation and the niceties of changes in pronunciation as fruitful ground. Above all, the questions it raises suggest several potentially fascinating new avenues of inquiry.

Luke Seaber,
University College London

Cold War Culture: Intellectuals, the Media and the Practice of History

Jim Smyth

I. B. Tauris, London, 2016 pp 244

ISBN 978 1 78453 112 6

Jim Smyth is the author of a fine study of Irish radicalism in the late eighteenth century, *The Men of No Property* (1998). Pursuing this interest, he began work on a biography of the historian Lewis Namier who, for some years, had dominated eighteenth century studies. As he admits, this project was prompted 'for mainly negative reasons' (p. 1). While a biography of Namier written from a critical perspective would certainly be worthwhile, we can all be grateful that the project metamorphosed into *Cold War Culture*, yet another outstanding book. Namier still figures prominently but as a symptom rather than as the patient. Nothing better captures the state of historical studies at our great universities at the height of the Cold War than Smyth's account of the country's most eminent historians meeting at Trinity College, Cambridge, to discuss 'the nascent *History of Parliament*' and spending a whole afternoon furiously debating whether the words 'Queen of England' should be capitalised or not. An outraged Namier made his position clear: 'I will not have my Queen with a small q' (p. 9). Those were the days.

Smyth uses the practice of history in Britain in the 1950s as a way into the exploration of Cold War culture. According to Eric Hobsbawm, after 1948 no known communist got a position or, if already in place, promotion in a British university for at least a decade. Hobsbawm himself had the uncomfortable experience of having the economic historian, Professor M. M. Postan, doing everything he could 'to thwart the professional progress of his former student' (p. 119). Underpinning this was the intellectual domination of the Namier school with the likes of Herbert Butterfield actually warning that its ascendancy was such that there was a danger of ending up with a 'historiographical *Nineteen Eighty-Four*', presumably with Namier as Big Brother. Indeed, by 1957 'Namier Inc' seemed to have a secure domination, one is tempted to use the word 'hegemony', over the field (pp 80, 129). From this point of view, the Namierite ascendancy was a historical reflex of the End of Ideology, projecting into the past the belief that ideas were of no political importance, that the conflict of ideas had been won, settled once and for all. As Smyth amusingly points out, these people considered royalism as above ideology!

This discussion is extremely interesting in its own right, but there is much more of interest in *Cold War Culture*. Inevitably, George Orwell puts in an appearance with the acknowledgement that

Nineteen Eighty-Four 'did more, by far than any other book, fictional or non-fictional, to popularize the concept, and warn against the consequences of totalitarianism'. As Smyth insists, 'Orwell's writings ... resonated powerfully in the political and literary culture of the 1950s' (p. 13). Nevertheless, there are some problems with Smyth's discussion of Orwell. We are seriously told, for example, that Orwell's politics derived not from his reading of political literature, but from 'his celebration of Englishness', an Englishness that he reduces to 'its defining characteristic – decency' (p. 15). First of all, of course, this leaves out the importance of experience, of his time as a policeman in Burma, of his service with the P. O. U. M. militia in Spain, of his time working as a propagandist at the BBC and so on. But it also seriously underestimates the importance of his reading, of his search for answers to political questions. His experiences in Spain, for example, led to a search for an explanation for the communists' actions and, as a corollary, what sort of society was the Soviet Union if it demanded such behaviour. Was it a socialist society at all? It was this search that led him down the road to *Nineteen Eighty-Four*. The importance of Orwell's relationship with the US journal *Partisan Review*, both as a writer and as a reader, is completely neglected.

REVIEW

Smyth is on surer ground with his insistence that Orwell's objection to totalitarianism came from the perspective of 'the democratic left'. While he mistakenly repeats the accusation that Orwell supplied British intelligence with the names of the politically suspect, he nevertheless does argue that if he had lived and been well enough, he would still probably not have attended the 1950 Congress for Cultural Freedom conference in Berlin. His explanation for this is not altogether convincing however: 'Orwell would surely have recoiled in distaste from such un-English stridency' (p. 12). Indeed, Smyth seriously argues more generally that Britain avoided all 'the excesses of McCarthyite loyalty oaths, blacklists and witchhunts' because of the country's 'innate moderation' (p. 12). While British political culture was certainly different from that of the United States, a good case can be made that if the Labour Party had been re-elected in 1951 then we might well have seen the blossoming of something approaching a fully-fledged British McCarthyism courtesy of Clement Attlee. Having defeated the Left in the broadest sense, the incoming Churchill government did not feel any need to go down this road and was also less subordinate to the United States than the Labour government had been.

One of *Cold War Culture's* great strengths is its account of the fraying of consensus in Britain and of some of the individuals involved. There is the compulsory nod to the 'Angry Young Men', although as Smyth insists they were a myth, a creation of the press, an episode in 'the history of modern publicity' more than anything else (p. 88). His discussion of the campaign against capital punishment as presaging the turning tide is particularly interesting with Victor Gollancz, Arthur Koestler and others setting up the National Campaign for the Abolition of Capital Punishment in 1955. And, of course, the following year there was the Anglo-French invasion of Egypt and the Russian invasion of Hungary.

The disastrous Suez invasion was ridden out by the Conservatives, but the Hungarian intervention had a tremendous impact on the Communist Party and not just on the intellectuals, and on the fellow-travelling Left. Khruschev's revelations regarding the nature of Stalin's rule in the Soviet Union were reinforced by the Hungarian invasion in the most damaging way possible. This trauma opened the way for the emergence of the New Left. The context for the emergence of the New Left was provided by the Campaign for Nuclear Disarmament in 1958, which Smyth describes as 'the largest, most passionate, extra-parliamentary protest movement since the days of the Suffragettes' (p. 148). All this is laid out extremely well. And there are excellent discussions of the work of Richard Hoggart, Raymond Williams and E. P. Thompson.

One point that one cannot criticise Smyth for neglecting because it is not necessary for his argument but that is worth some mention is the New Left's determined rejection of Orwell as an inspiration. His posthumous conscription as a Cold Warrior probably accounts for part of this, but that certainly does not seem enough to account for E. P. Thompson's shabby, indeed, thoroughly dishonest treatment of Orwell in his 'Outside the Whale' essay first published in 1960. Was this because Orwell had rejected Stalinism too early and stood as some sort of personal indictment of those who had needed to be told of Stalin's crimes by the Russians before they would believe in them? Whatever the reason, the New Left's attitude towards George Orwell needs further exploration. This stance has continued down to the present day with that excellent journal *New Left Review*, for example, resolutely ignoring the man and his politics.

To return to Smyth's book, it clearly gives the reader considerable food for thought. Well-written, persuasively argued, and coming at its topic in interesting new ways, it is to be highly recommended

John Newsinger,
Bath Spa University

Espionage and Exile: Fascism and Anti-Fascism in British Spy Fiction and Film

Phyllis Lassner

Edinburgh University Press, Edinburgh, 2016 pp 272

ISBN 9781474401104 (hbk); 9781474416733 (ePub); 9781474401111 (PDF)

What is the point of espionage fiction? Like any popular genre, it exists partly to entertain, but no other fictional genre is as overtly political. Spies cross international frontiers, confront geopolitical enemies, risk their lives for governmental institutions – so fictional spies cannot help but get themselves involved in political questions. From its emergence in nineteenth-century British invasion-scare fiction, the espionage genre has served an immediate ideological purpose – to legitimise those actions and methods, including some usually considered to be reprehensible, that are held to be necessary for defending the realm. From William le Queux's Duckworth Drew to John le Carré's George Smiley, fictional spies are shown as necessary if often unpalatable instruments of national defence.

Orwell observed in 'Boys' Weeklies' (1940) that, 'in England, popular imaginative literature is a field that left-wing thought has never begun to enter', and the espionage genre is sometimes characterised as conservative or reactionary by its very nature. The crime writer Val McDermid, for instance, has characterised the thriller as generally right-of-centre (while the detective story, often concerned with the socially marginalised, is generally left-wing). But as Phyllis Lassner argues in *Espionage and Exile: Fascism and Anti-Fascism in British Spy Fiction and Film*, the espionage thriller can also challenge dominant ideologies: the novels of writers such as Eric Ambler, Helen MacInnes, and John le Carré 'express the urge to provide counter-narratives to the casual prejudices, wilful ignorance and silences that constituted official and general responses to political and racialised victims of exile' (p. 221).

Although she does explore at some length the anti-establishment positions of Ambler in particular, her concern is more particularly with the victims of international order and disorder – and Jewish victims above all. As might be expected from a distinguished scholar in Holocaust and Jewish studies, Lassner focuses her book on characters who are either Jewish or who are fleeing persecution. She can therefore show that, at least from the 1930s to the Cold War, the genre was politically engaged not only on questions of national security but also on what we might term human security – the rights of individuals and peoples to live without fear of persecution.

The strength of Lassner's study lies in it being grounded in close textual study. For Orwell scholars, this book will be of greatest

REVIEW

interest for its chapters on writers of the 1930s and 1940s, and her examination of Ambler novels from that period is particularly detailed and comprehensive, productively linking Ambler's fascination with globalised capitalism to his horror at the rise of fascism and Nazism in Europe. Her best chapter, though, is on le Carré, not least as she finds in his first novel, *Call for the Dead* (1961), a case-study almost tailor-made for her argument in Elsa Fennan, a concentration camp survivor who is unmasked as a Soviet spy in the home counties. Her analysis of Elsa and of the Jewish characters in *The Spy Who Came in from the Cold* (1963) shows that much of the power of le Carré's early novels derives from his exploration of the Cold War as a legacy of the Second World War. Lassner also deserves praise for rescuing the neglected works of mid-century women writers. MacInnes is a recognised espionage novelist but Lassner also finds room for two others not normally associated with the genre, Pamela Frankau and Ann Bridge. Together, Lassner argues that these women writers deepen the genre by diverting it from its traditional action-orientation towards ethical choices and psychological exploration.

This is, then, a valuable and interesting study, which amply succeeds in bringing to prominence the more subaltern figures of the genre – characters and authors. It is also a frustrating one, and its principal weakness lies in its selection of cases. Lassner finds interesting and important things to say about all the novelists she covers, as well as the actor and film-maker Leslie Howard, who gets a chapter of his own – but the method of selecting them is, by Lassner's own admission, impressionistic: 'My rationale for this selection derives from my own reading and film-going experiences, when I began to notice that the figure of the exiled Jew and other refugees kept appearing in the 1930s fictions of Eric Ambler and Pamela Frankau, the 1940s fictions by Helen MacInnes and Ann Bridge and filmmaker Leslie Howard, and in the Cold War novels by Frankau and John le Carre' (pp 2-3).

Between them, these seven authors cover four decades and two wars, two mediums (the novel and film), and even a range of genres: Lassner acknowledges that her examination of Frankau's *The Devil We Know* (1939) 'might seem an anomaly in this book' and Frankau's novel 'would certainly not be found on any canonical list of spy fiction' (p. 71). There are a couple of problems that result from this eclectic approach. The first is a lack of coherence: by moving from a novel set in the Second World War but written in 1953 (Ann Bridge's *A Place to Stand*) to Powell and Pressburger's 1941 film *49th Parallel* (which starred Leslie Howard and who contributed his own scripted dialogue), or from Jewish characters to more general discussions of the political content of her chosen novels, this begins to look like a book without a clear focus. The second problem is the reliability of her conclusions: Lassner asserts throughout that her observations apply to espionage fiction in general, but she has taken a small sample and left out a great deal of work, some of which would support her argument and much that would refute it – Greene's *The Confidential Agent* or Geoffrey Household's *Rogue Male* (both 1939) would fit within her thesis, while the work of, say, Ian Fleming would provide much evidence that espionage fiction, like any genre, is multi-dimensional.

A more rigorous selection – focusing solely on Jewish characters in espionage fiction, or employing a narrower date-range, or opting for a more ambitious selection that encompassed many more writers – would have yielded a clearer focus and hence a more authoritative result. As it is, Lassner's judgments can really only be said to apply to the few authors she has examined, not the genre as a whole.

It is sadly rather common for literary-critical monographs by established scholars to be written in prose that is so laden with abstractions and vaguely-expressed concepts, that any line of argument or conclusive point becomes all but impossible to follow or discern. Lassner is a model of Orwellian clarity in comparison to some of Eng.Lit's worst offenders, but I still found her judgments slippery and her arguments elusive. Take, for instance, her opening salvo: 'This book will examine the narrative interweave of spy fiction and exile to show how each is a political discourse and critically heuristic perspective that illuminates the other' (p. 2). How can a genre and a topic constitute a 'narrative interweave'? In what way is exile 'a political discourse', or a 'critically heuristic perspective'? And how can it be both of these very different things at the same time? It is a shame that a fairly straightforward assertion – that spy fiction from the 1930s to 1960s tends to be interested in the condition of exile for reasons which are politically significant – should be blurred rather than revealed by the author's prose, a mass of literary critical buzzwords falling on the judgment like soft snow.

Andrew Glazzard,
Royal United Services Institute

REVIEW

George Orwell Studies

Subscription information
Each volume contains two issues, published half-yearly.

Annual Subscription (including postage)

Personal Subscription

UK	£25
Europe	£28
RoW	£30

Institutional Subscription

UK	£100
Europe	£115
RoW	£120

Single Issue copies (subject to availability)

UK	£15
Europe	£17
RoW	£20

Enquiries regarding subscriptions and orders should be sent to:

Journals Fulfilment Department
Abramis Academic
ASK House
Northgate Avenue
Bury St Edmunds
Suffolk, IP32 6BB
UK

Tel: +44(0)1284 700321
Email: info@abramis.co.uk

www.ingramcontent.com/pod-product-compliance
Lightning Source LLC
Chambersburg PA
CBHW080407170426
43193CB00016B/2844